SCHOLASTIC

W9-BVJ-034

RAISING ★ A ROCK-STAR ★ READER

75 Quick Tips to Help Your Child Develop a Lifelong Love of Reading

New York • Toronto • London • Auckland • Sydney
Mexico City • New Delhi • Hong Kong • Buenos Aires

Dedication

*To my mom and dad, for filling our house with books and raising four rock-star readers;
to my husband, Brent, my inspiring, tireless supporter; and to Maddy, Owen, and Cora,
the three coolest kids on the planet and the only reason teachmama.com exists.* **–Amy Mascott**

*To my husband Jason, without whom all the best things wouldn't be possible, to all my students who
have taught me new ways to reach understanding, and most importantly, to my two children who inspire me
to be a better teacher and mom every day.* **–Allison McDonald**

Photo Credits: Photos ©: cover: Aidon/Getty Images; cover: firemanYU/iStockphoto; 5: Christopher Futcher/
iStockphoto; 7: pixdeluxe/iStockphoto; 9: Stuart Pearce/Getty Images; 11: wavebreakmedia/Shutterstock, Inc.;
15: Roberto Westbrook/Getty Images; 17: Carey Kirkella/Getty Images; 19: Photo_Concepts/iStockphoto;
23: JGI/Tom Grill/Getty Images; 25: Fairfax Media via Getty Images; 27: GlobalStock/iStockphoto; 29:
digitalskillet/iStockphoto; 31: Svetlana Braun/iStockphoto; 34: Christopher Futcher/iStockphoto; 37 top:
kenny1/Shutterstock, Inc.; 37 bottom: Tagstock1/iStockphoto; 48: AMR Image/iStockphoto; 54: PonyWang/
iStockphoto; 57: Monkey Business Images/Shutterstock, Inc.; 62: pixinoo/Shutterstock, Inc.; 67: Chris
Bernard/Getty Images; 72: Datacraft Co Ltd/Getty Images; 74: pavla/Shutterstock, Inc.; 78: Peter Muller/
Getty Images; 82: Ruth Jenkinson/Getty Images; 83: Claire Bock/Getty Images; 93: ansazan/iStockphoto;
95: Studio Tec/a.collectionRF; 106: PeopleImages.com/Getty Images; 108: Juriah Mosin/Shutterstock, Inc.;
112: Sergey Nivens/Shutterstock, Inc.; 114: Marc Romanelli/Getty Images; 116: Blend Images/Shutterstock,
Inc.; 117: KidStock/Getty Images; 119: Hemant Mehta/Getty Images; 120: Rob Van Petten/Getty Images;
123: JGI/Jamie Gri/Getty Images; 125: Jekaterina Nikitina/Getty Images; All other photos © Amy Mascott
and Allison McDonald

Cover design by Tannaz Fassihi

Interior design by Holly Grundon

ISBN: 978-0-545-80617-6

Copyright © 2015 by Amy Mascott and Allison McDonald

Printed in the U.S.A.

3 4 5 6 7 8 9 10   23   20 19

CONTENTS

About the Authors

Amy Mascott, M.A., Reading; B.A., English Education

Founder and editor of Teach Mama

Amy Mascott is the creator of teachmama.com, where since 2008, she has shared tools and resources parents can use to become the best teachers they can be for their children. A reading specialist, writer, and literacy consultant, Amy's work has been featured in dozens of online and print publications, including Scholastic Parents, PBS Parents, PBS Digital Studios, readwritethink.org, and more. A former high school English teacher, Amy has expanded the walls of her classroom to share her expertise at local and national conferences and events. Married to an elementary school principal, Amy resides in the DC Metro area with her three crazy-cool kids, a dog, two birds, and four fish.

Allison McDonald, B.A., History; B.Ed., Elementary Education

Founder and editor of No Time For Flash Cards

Allison McDonald is a preschool teacher and the mom behind the popular early education website notimeforflashcards.com. Reading, especially helping to lay the groundwork for learning to read, has been a passion of Allison's for many years. While studying elementary education at Lakehead University in Thunder Bay, Ontario, she worked as a reading tutor and volunteered with Pioneer College as a buddy reader for underprivileged children. Once she started her teaching career, she fell even more in love with getting children excited about learning to read through hands-on activities. When she paused her teaching career to start her own family, she started the website *No Time For Flash Cards* and over the next many years, filled it with hands-on activities to help parents and teachers. Allison began writing the *Raise a Reader* blog on Scholastic Parents in 2012. Now that she is back in a classroom, she is eager to have a chance to help even more children fall in love with books.

INTRODUCTION

Reading is our thing. But we totally get that it might not be yours.

So because we *love* reading, and because we are continually amazed, in awe, and humbled by the process of reading acquisition—how kids learn to read and become better readers—we want to help you.

With just a few minutes a day, a few times a day, no matter where you are, as a parent, you can help your child become a strong reader—even if you don't consider yourself one. We want to help you because we know we can. More importantly, we know you can. It's easier than you think. It's possible. Trust us.

The crazy thing is that even *before* children are able to read texts on their own, they can develop a lot of skills that will build a strong foundation for literacy—just by being read aloud to by an adult.

You are your child's first—and most important!—teacher.

> We've got plenty of tips outlining simple things you can do to get the most out of reading aloud to your child.

So whether it's you, or Grandpa, or even the babysitter doing the reading, a read-aloud can help your child:

★ Learn how to handle a book (Finding the front cover and turning the pages from right to left doesn't come naturally!)

★ Become aware of letters, words, and sounds

★ Build vocabulary

★ Follow the flow of a story

★ Develop his or her attention span

★ And so much more!

In addition to reading aloud, we'll share other everyday activities you can do to help your child build the foundation for one of the most important skills he or she will ever have: reading.

Reading is tough. It's an active process, which means that while you're reading, you're working. And you are working *hard*. You might not realize it, but reading takes a lot of energy:

★ Your brain is busy decoding, or figuring out how to pronounce the words that the groups of letters on the page create.

★ You're pulling together what you know about the sounds the letters make when they're together and what the word they create means.

★ You're merging that word together with what the words around it mean so that you can make sense of the phrase, sentence, and paragraph.

★ You're also crazy busy *thinking*. You're making connections between what you know and what the story or text is telling you.

★ You're asking questions in your mind about plot, characters, and setting.

★ You're making predictions, guesses about what may or may not happen.

★ You're synthesizing and inferring—trying to bring together all that you know about a subject and combining it with what you're reading. Then you're creating new meaning based on that information.

★ You're building your fluency, which is reading in a way that sounds natural, like talking.

All the while? You're trying to enjoy it. Find pleasure in it. Relax with it and have fun with it, so that you are carried away, even for a short while, to places as far off and mysterious as Willy Wonka's Chocolate Factory or as familiar as Ramona's living room.

Really, reading is no cakewalk— but we can help you make learning to read more of a treat for your child.

For years now, we've poured everything we have into writing our blogs, sharing ways that parents can take a more active role in their kids' early learning. And for years we've co-written *Scholastic Parents: Raise a Reader* blog, sharing everything parents need to know about—wait for it—raising kids who read!

We've finally decided to answer a ton of requests from friends, family, and community members and put our ideas together in a quick and easy read. Something you can take with you just about anywhere— the park, backyard, playroom, waiting room, car, metro—anywhere. Something you can pull out whenever you want to fill five minutes here or there with an activity that really counts.

We're not guaranteeing miracles here, but what we are sure of is that if we can do it, *anyone* can do it. And every little bit counts. Everything. We promise. Your kids will thank you for it one day.

A HOUSE OF BOOKS

A few minutes here and there is all you need to set the stage for a seriously literate environment.

Let's get literate!

Everything you need to know to turn your home into a literate environment for your baby, toddler, preschooler, or school-aged child is here—from the must-have books for your kids' bookshelves to the secrets to creating a home where kids are excited about literacy and reading.

You may be wondering when is the best time to introduce your child to books and reading, and the answer is—from Day One. Seriously. What better way to rock baby to sleep than by singing lullabies, chanting nursery rhymes, retelling a fairy tale, or reading from a beloved picture book. But if you didn't start then, not to worry—you can start now. It's never too late!

CREATE A LIBRARY FROM DAY ONE.

Create a fun, book-loving environment by stocking your shelves with just the right books. So much of parenting is about setting up buffets for your kids. The same way you may offer three different choices at a meal, hoping your child will tolerate two out of the three, offering many book choices for children, even for babies, is important.

When you are looking for books for your infant, you want to look for these five basic features:

Sturdy construction. Board books are perfect, and they will last well into your child's preschool years. They aren't just for babies.

Bright colors with high contrast. Infants will be drawn to primary colors and contrast. Find books with lots of bright colors or stick with just black and white.

A melodic text. Babies love to be sung to, and books with text that sounds like a song are great for babies who find comfort in repetitive, gentle sounds.

A story you like. Repetition is comforting to children, so as your baby grows, you will probably read his favorite book hundreds of times before he can read it to himself. It may as well be one you like.

Interactive elements. Textures, tabs, flaps to lift—all of these won't be used right away, but as your baby grows, she will appreciate these features. When children get to the stage where sitting still for a book is near impossible, interactive elements will keep them engaged and interested!

TIP #2 STOCK YOUR LIBRARY WITH THESE TOP 10 BOOKS FOR BABIES.

Reading to your baby is such a gift, and children are never too young to be read to—anytime, and especially at bedtime. From the start, make reading a part of winding down the day, and it will stick. Reading together will become as routine as teeth-brushing, but a lot more fun!

Here are ten top-notch books to read to your baby.

1. ***Moo, Baa, La La La!*** by Sandra Boynton
    This book will turn the most serious reader into a silly reader and get your baby giggling with you. Humor is a wonderful thing, and this book makes reading fun.

2. ***Goodnight Moon*** by Margaret Wise Brown
    This book's lullaby-like text matched with the simple illustrations will help your baby wind down from a busy day.

3. ***Learn the Alphabet With Northwest Coast Native Art*** by Ryan Cranmer (and others) Allison found this book at a gas station, and it remains the very best thing she has ever bought at a gas station. The artwork is bright and bold, perfect for babies.

4. ***Ten Little Fingers and Ten Little Toes*** by Mem Fox Babies love seeing themselves in books, and this book shows lots of babies for your little one to admire and count.

5. ***Where Is Baby's Belly Button?*** by Karen Katz Labeling body parts will come naturally later in development, but this book lets kids read and explore the human body in an age-appropriate way.

6. ***Brown Bear, Brown Bear*** by Bill Martin, Jr. This book can be used with any age group from birth through early elementary, but babies especially love the bold illustrations and the soothing, repetitive text.

7. ***Everywhere Babies*** by Susan Meyers Every kind of family is depicted in this book. From same-sex parents to single dads, grandparents as caregivers to multi-ethnic families, this inclusive book with countless babies is a great one for babies to grow with.

8. ***Quiet LOUD*** by Leslie Patricelli This is a book about opposites that babies will adore. The illustrations are simple but hilarious, and babies love seeing the naughty things that the baby in the book does.

9. ***Good Night, Gorilla*** by Peggy Rathmann
   This wordless book is a favorite of many children, including our own. The animals follow the zookeeper home, and even after his wife escorts the animals back to the zoo, the sneaky little ape finds his way back into the bed with the zookeeper and his wife. Because it's wordless, you can tell the story very quickly or stretch it out, depending on the child.

10. ***That's Not My Puppy . . . Its Coat Is Too Hairy*** by Fionna Watt
    This little book is a great choice for babies who are exploring textures. Each page includes a new texture to feel. Books like these are great for active babies who might prefer to experience the world than read about it.

TIP #3 — SHARE THESE TOP 10 BOOKS FOR TODDLERS.

Toddlers are technically children who are just learning to walk, but when we think of a toddler, we think of newfound independence, strong opinions, running feet, stamping feet, demands to be held, demands to be let go, and quiet cuddles. Toddlers are a special blend of baby and child, and the books that are best suited for them reflect that.

These books are dynamic and perfect for active toddlers. Some encourage movement, some have flaps to lift and textures to feel, and some are perfect for verbal interaction and conversation.

1. **Doggies** by Sandra Boynton
   This simple counting book will appeal to all toddlers, but especially to dog lovers. As always, Boynton's great humor shines through the words and illustrations.

2. **Clap Your Hands** by Lorinda Bryan Cauley
   Adding movement to reading time with toddlers is a great way to include them as active participants, not just a passive audience. *Clap Your Hands* is a great one to get up and move along to, combining reading and action.

3. **From Head to Toe** by Eric Carle (You can't go wrong with anything from Eric Carle.)
   This is another great book to get kids moving as you read.

4. **Chicka Chicka ABC** by Bill Martin Jr. and John Archambault
   This is a wonderful little alphabet book featuring upper- and lowercase letters and a rhythmic, melodic text.

5. **We're Going on a Bear Hunt** by Helen Oxenbury
   You can read this one snuggled up together or act it out as you go.

6. **One Duck Stuck** by Phyllis Root
   Counting and teamwork come together in this book, which was a big favorite in Allison's toddler classroom years ago. It's also become a recent family favorite.

7. **Mr. Brown Can Moo! Can You?** by Dr. Seuss
   It's never too early to rhyme with your children. Playing with letter sounds through rhyme is a great way to explore language with toddlers.

8. ***Dinosaur Roar!*** by Paul and Henrietta Stickland
    Opposites are featured using dinosaurs for appeal and humor in this fun board book.

9. ***Owl Babies*** by Martin Waddell
    Separation anxiety usually peaks in the toddler years, and this book is a great tool to let toddlers know that it's perfectly normal to miss their caregivers while they are apart.

10. ***Trashy Town*** by Andrea Zimmerman and David Clemesha
    We have never met a toddler who wasn't at least a little bit fascinated with the garbage truck. Readers get to go along with Mr. Gillie as he cleans up Trashy Town in this delightful book.

TIP #4 READ THESE TOP 10 BOOKS FOR PRESCHOOLERS.

When we think about reading with preschoolers, we think about choosing high-interest books—stories that spark discussion after reading and that have engaging illustrations and repetition of language to support children's developing literacy skills. We also seek out stories that make kids laugh because this is a critical time to make reading fun!

Check out these ten books for a solid foundation for your preschooler's home library.

1. **The Very Hungry Caterpillar** by Eric Carle
   If by chance you have not read this book, it's about a caterpillar who, you may have guessed, is really hungry. He eats some good things and some bad things, and there are consequences. This book is a wonderful introduction to healthy food choices and to the butterfly life cycle.

2. **Whoever You Are** by Mem Fox
   This book is a sweet look at the things all people have in common. The gentle text explains that even though we may look different from others or speak different languages, our hearts are the same.

3. **Something From Nothing** by Phoebe Gilman
   This book is a lesson in resourcefulness, which all children can use. The loving relationship between a little boy and his grandfather is front and center, and little readers adore the secondary story about the little mice who live under the floorboards of the house.

4. **Tacky the Penguin** by Helen Lester
   Tacky is an odd bird. He doesn't fit in, and sometimes the other penguins aren't very nice to him. That doesn't stop Tacky from being who he is. This lesson is one that children of this age can relate to and need to hear. Preschoolers are starting to experience the feeling of being self-conscious and will relate to Tacky and this funny book.

5. **The Paper Bag Princess** by Robert Munsch
   Elizabeth is a princess who loves Prince Ronald and goes to great lengths to save him when he is taken away by a dragon. After she saves the day, Ronald is less than grateful. Elizabeth stands up for herself and skips off into the sunset alone and happy. In the 20-plus years that Allison has been reading this book to groups of children, she has never had a child not like it; it is perhaps her favorite picture book ever.

It was incredibly difficult to shorten our favorite list to ten titles because there are so many great picture books out there.

6. ***The Kissing Hand*** by Audrey Penn

   Chester isn't so sure about going to school without his Mama. Most children can relate to not being ready to separate from Mom or Dad and the resulting feelings of anxiety. This book addresses those worries in an entertaining way and helps put words to feelings that young children often have a hard time expressing.

7. ***Where the Wild Things Are*** by Maurice Sendak

   Max is sent to his room because he was being wild, and after closing his door, he imagines a world that is free from parents and discipline, where he is king. This book is the epitome of childhood, and it taps into children's desire to control their environment. In the end, Max is drawn back home where he realizes he is loved best of all, even if he's not the king.

8. ***No, David!*** by David Shannon

   David is a troublemaker, but like many of our own little troublemakers, he is just being a kid and pushing the boundaries that can sometimes feel very unfair. We love this book because it's a wonderful way to talk about expectations, rules, and why they exist without having a big serious discussion with a 4-year-old. The fact that it's really funny helps, too.

9. ***Alexander and the Terrible, Horrible, No Good, Very Bad Day*** by Judith Viorst

   Some days are bad, and this is a lesson we all need to learn so that we can find our own ways to push through and start again in the morning. This book is a modern classic because it's brilliant. It was a childhood favorite of Allison's, and as a parent, she would pull it out when she could tell her kids needed a gentle reminder that some days are going to be terrible, horrible, no good, very bad days.

10. ***Don't Let the Pigeon Drive the Bus!*** by Mo Willems

When you ask a child about this book, the first thing he or she will say is how funny it is. And it's true—this book is hilarious. The fun of this book isn't just humor, it's also in reading with expression. The pigeon is rather emotional, especially when he doesn't get his way. Reading this book aloud to your child gives you a chance to model how to read with expression. As your child's reading ability develops, reading picture books like this will serve as a wonderful tool for mastering expression.

TIP #5

GROW YOUR LIBRARY WITH THESE TOP 10 BOOKS FOR KINDERGARTNERS.

Here's where the fun really begins. When kids begin kindergarten, we really want them to hit the ground running, which is why we spend so much time, effort, and energy doing what we can to build a solid foundation for them from birth up to this point.

Kindergarten is an important year for so many reasons. Kids will be very busy during the day meeting friends, learning to read, playing with numbers, and more, so they'll definitely need their downtime when they come home. Reading in the evenings, especially before bedtime, is something that parents will want to continue during the school year.

Not only will this bedtime routine allow you some meaningful one-on-one time with your growing child, it will also give you a chance to sneak in a little bit of worthwhile cuddle and reading time.

1. **Chrysanthemum** by Kevin Henkes
    Important topics like friendship, strength, and
    individuality are covered in this book about a
    mouse starting school.

2. **Dinosaur Dinosaur** by Kevin Lewis
    Follow along for a day in the life of Dinosaur,
    and you'll be on a rhythmic, rhyming ride.

3. **If You Give a Mouse a Cookie**
    by Laura Numeroff
    One thing leads to another, which leads to yet
    another, when you give Mouse a cookie. Kids
    love the chain of events and find it fun to see
    how it goes full circle.

4. **Today I Feel Silly & Other Moods That Make My Day**
    by Jamie Lee Curtis
    Learning how to identify and explain feelings is an important skill
    for children, and they will surely see themselves in this book that
    chronicles the ups and downs of everyday life.

5. **Sometimes I Like to Curl Up in a Ball**
    by Vicki Churchill
    Beautiful images of Wombat and his friends grace the pages
    of this book, which is an ideal, melodic bedtime story for kids
    of all ages.

6. **Arnie the Doughnut** by Laurie Keller
    What happens when your doughnut stops you mid-bite and begs
    you to not eat him? Thanks to Arnie, children will never look at
    things quite the same way again.

Children ages 6-11 who are frequent readers (reading books 5-7 days a week)

- have been read aloud to early and often
- spend less time online
- have parents who are frequent readers

(*Kids & Family Reading Report*, Scholastic, 2014)

7. **The Red Book** by Barbara Lehman
This Caldecott Award winner tells a complex and interesting story without a single word. It is guaranteed to get kids thinking in totally new ways.

8. **Art & Max** by David Wiesner
A book that kids will want to read over and over, *Art & Max* tells the story of an experienced artist and his novice pal through minimal text and thought-provoking illustrations.

9. **The Gardener** by Sarah Stewart
Told through a series of letters between Lydia Grace Finch and her parents, this story shares a girl's experience living in the city with her uncle during the Depression. Readers will be moved by her strength, determination, and kindness.

10. **Zen Shorts** by Jon J. Muth
This Caldecott Honor book has a complicated but discussion-worthy story with a message that will definitely resonate with youngsters.

BONUS

The Berenstain Bears books by Stan and Jan Berenstain
Kids love to "conquer" book series; that is, they love to try to find them all, read them all, and really know them all. This series covers everything from friendship to school to peer pressure to family conflict, and each book provides kids with a take-away life lesson.

The Arthur books by Marc Brown
In this series, Arthur experiences everything from the worst family vacation to a chatty little sister to a baby brother who won't stop crying—things kids *and* adults can relate to.

ENCOURAGE INDEPENDENT READING WITH THESE TOP 10 EARLY CHAPTER BOOKS.

TIP #6

Once your child starts reading independently, sharing series books is a great way to keep the momentum going. Since the main characters are the same across a series, readers have the comfort of knowing what to expect and are motivated to read more about their favorite characters. Here are some tried-and-true favorites:

1. **Nate the Great series**
   by Marjorie Weinman Shermat
   Super books for kids who are just ready for chapter books, Nate the Great will take readers on many mysteries and adventures.

2. **The Puppy Place series** by Ellen Miles
   Especially for animal lovers, The Puppy Place series not only spreads a message about the importance of caring for animals, but also teaches about friendship, family, and giving.

3. **A to Z Mysteries** by Ron Roy
   Kids love the fact that there is a mystery for each letter of the alphabet, and they connect with the characters Dink, Josh, and Ruth Rose. (If your child loves mysteries, also check out The Capital Mysteries, which take place in our nation's capital and feature K.C. Corcoran and Marshall Li, as well as The Calendar Mysteries, which feature the younger siblings of Dink, Josh, and Ruth Rose. The Calendar Mysteries are actually a great place for readers to begin, as they're geared toward first and second graders.)

4. **Flat Stanley series** by Jeff Brown
    Flat Stanley has been around for years now, with various adaptations and extensions, because who doesn't really love reading about a flat boy?

5. **Ivy & Bean series** by Annie Barrows
    Ivy and Bean are two friends who prove that opposites do attract!

6. **The Rainbow Magic series** by Daisy Meadows
    There are so many books in this series that once kids get hooked, they've got reading material for months.

7. **Captain Awesome series** by Stan Kirby and George O'Connor
    Younger readers will totally appreciate the larger type and illustrations that support them as they follow the adventures of 8-year-old Eugene McGillicudy, a.k.a. Captain Awesome.

8. **The Magic Treehouse series** by Mary Pope Osborne
    Jack and Annie travel through time and across the world and back in this series that involves mystery, science, history, and magic.

9. **The Geronimo Stilton series** by Geronimo Stilton
    These graphic novels are told from newspaper reporter Geronimo's point of view, and they include a fun cast of characters who each have their own series. Tons of illustrations, funky print and fonts, and variety on each page keep readers engaged.

10. **The Ramona books** by Beverly Cleary
    Ramona Quimby is a character that many children can relate to or at least appreciate for her humor, honesty, and follies. Like many kids, Ramona must deal with family, school, and friend issues, all the while making sure she's a well-behaved young girl. Not always easy.

TIP #7 — CREATE A ROCK-SOLID BEDTIME ROUTINE WITH READING AT ITS HEART.

Establishing any routine takes more than a few minutes, but the decision to create a routine only takes a second. Creating a predictable bedtime reading routine is the easiest and most important step to creating a literate environment for your family.

Here are a few tips that have made the bedtime book routine a cinch for our families:

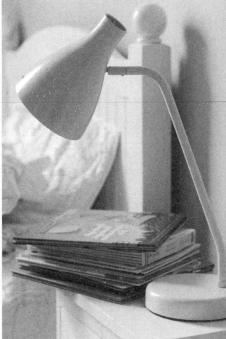

Start when your child is an infant. If you haven't started yet, start tonight. Children are never too little, and it's never too late.

Take reading time into account when you are establishing bedtimes. If you are antsy for your child to just hurry up and get to sleep, reading will be rushed and anything but stress-free. Be sure to plan accordingly so you can give yourself and your child time to explore and enjoy the material.

Make firm rules about how many books or chapters you are going to read. At Allison's house, the magic number is three. But find what works for you, and when you do, stick with it. Bedtime negotiations are never fun. The last thing we want to do is make the experience anxiety-filled, which will cause children to relate reading with stress and anger.

Have a book box or special place for bedtime books. It saves time if you don't have to hunt books down after a long day.

Let your child choose the books, and mix it up with magazines, nonfiction, and comics, too!

CREATE A BOOK NOOK.

A book nook is a fun (and motivating) place for kids to read. Have you seen some of the book nooks on Pinterest? There are creative people out there! This trick may not be worthy of Pinterest, but it will help your kids read more. Creating a book nook doesn't mean buying new shelves and spending mega-bucks on decorations. A book nook can be as simple as a cozy corner with a basket of books. The trick is making it special.

Some ways you can turn an everyday spot in your home into a functional book nook for your child include providing:

A comfy place to sit *other than* your child's bed. Even though we often read bedtime books in our children's beds, sleep experts suggest that beds only be used for sleep, especially for children who have a hard time sleeping. Instead, choose a special chair, comfy corner with pillows, or window seat. An unused crib mattress with a few throw pillows makes great seating.

A quiet spot, separate from the noise and action in the home. Allison only has two kids, and she feels her house is a zoo some days—and more kids means even more activity. We know that if we want our kids to have a cozy place just for reading, it needs to be removed from the frenetic action of a family home. A corner of a bedroom, playroom, or even a foyer can be a great place for a little book nook. During the summer, an outdoor book nook is a great way to encourage your kids to read.

Easy access to books. A low bookshelf, a big basket, rain-gutter shelves on the wall—no matter what you choose, make sure that books are within reach. It's faster to clean up, and more importantly, it's easier for your little book lover to grab a book, then another, then another!

Good lighting. We are trying to make reading as wonderful as possible for our children, and one way to do that is to literally put books into the best light possible. We want to bring those illustrations to life and focus on the words—not on the game system that is waiting for them downstairs.

TIP #9 MAKE BOOKS A BIGGER PART OF YOUR CHILD'S WORLD.

Learning to read is something many kids need some motivation to get through—start to finish. There are a number of ways to spark their interest, but one of the simplest ways is to make reading fun by bringing their favorite books to life.

Don't worry—we are not talking about acting them out. (Unless you want to.)

You can bring books to life in *lots* of ways. You can use characters from books as inspiration for Halloween costumes, throw birthday parties with your child's favorite book as the theme (pssst ... check Pinterest for specific ideas. Trust us, you'll find some!), or give book-themed gifts.

Allison's son had a children's book-themed nursery, and all his first stuffed animals and artwork featured characters from beloved children's books. When he was old enough to recognize them in books, he had an instant connection. He'd been falling asleep looking at Max from *Where the Wild Things Are* his whole life, and it's still one of his favorite books.

You can watch movies or go to theater productions based on books after you read them, and—yes—you can even read books based on your child's favorite cartoon.

One of our favorite ways to bring books to life is to make up stories about our favorite characters. The familiar characters act as storytelling prompts, and as we make up our own stories based on these characters, children make more lasting connections to them—and as a side benefit, this promotes reading, too!

Filling your home with books and making reading a part of your daily routine provide a solid foundation for your child's literacy growth. Read on for the next layer of literacy—talking!

CHAPTER 2

TALK TO ME, KID

No. More. Baby. Talk.

There. We said it. Sure, a comforting voice that is loving and kind is great, but really . . . adults speaking baby talk is hard for other adults to hear, and it doesn't do a lick for kids. You may think it's cute and adorable to hear your two-year-old call *strawberries* "stwaahbewwies," but she needs to hear you pronounce words correctly and use the proper terms for things.

Children develop the ability to make the sounds of our language over time by listening to the adults in their world and by saying the words themselves. That's why talking with your kids is so important—it gives children lots of chances to hear and say words and to expand their vocabulary. The fancy term for this is *oral language*, and the simplest way to develop it is to talk with your child—a lot!

Please don't ever talk to your kids using baby words or baby terms.

All you need are five minutes here and there to set the stage for strong oral language skills for your kids.

Many parents worry about how their children pronounce certain words. But, as we'll share below, there's usually no need to worry—children's ability to produce specific speech sounds develops over time, and speech issues typically work themselves out by the time kids are eight years old.

Really. It's amazing. Just as they outgrow their cribs and sippy cups, most children eventually leave behind those adorable mispronunciations, all in good time.

 TIP #10 ## KNOW THAT SPEECH SOUNDS OFTEN DEVELOP OVER TIME.

When Amy learned that speech sounds were developmental, a humongous weight was lifted off of her chest—and we know many other parents feel the same way. *Developmental* just means that speech sounds happen for kids over time. They usually click in a certain progression, not all at once. Just as children master physical milestones, such as sitting up and walking at different ages, so it is with speech development.

So go ahead and keep the general timeframe for acquisition of speech sounds in your back pocket. And take a close look at year number eight. The tricky /r/ sound? Give your kids up through age 8 to really get it.

Here's a general timeline indicating the approximate age when your child should be saying certain sounds, just to set your mind at ease. Know that these ages are approximate and that there are slight variations between girls and boys.

Age 3: *b, h, m, p, w*; boys: *n*; girls: *d*

Age 4: all of the above and *f, g, k, t*; boys: *d*; girls: *j, n, y, kw, tw*

Age 5: all of the above and boys: *j, y*; girls: *l*

Age 6: all of the above and *v, bl, fl, gl, kl, pl*; girls: *ch, sh, th* (as in *thumb*); boys: *l, kw, tw*

Age 7: all of the above and *th* (as in *that*); boys: *ch, sh*

Age 8: all of the above and *r, br, dr, fr, gr, kr, pr, tr, zh* (as in *measure*); boys: *th* (as in *thumb*)

Age 9: all of the above and *s, ng, sk, sl, sm, sn, sp, st, sw, skw, spl, spr, str, skr*

Of course, some children do have speech problems, in which case early intervention is key. Some red flags to note:

- ★ If the child's peers can't understand him or her
- ★ If it has become a challenge for him or her to participate in school or social situations
- ★ If the child expresses distress about how he or she sounds

If you notice any of the above signs or think that something may be of real concern, talk to your child's teacher or ask your pediatrician for a referral for an evaluation. Most school districts provide speech therapy free of charge even before the child is in kindergarten.

Adapted from Smit, A., Hand, L., Freilinger, J., Bernthal, J., & Bird, A. (November 1990). The Iowa articulation norms project and its Nebraska replication. Journal of Speech and Hearing Disorders, 55, 779-798 and The Talking Child, www.talkingchild.com.

TIP #11 · DO. NOT. CORRECT. YOUR. CHILD'S. SPEECH.

Who feels good getting publicly corrected by another person? Not anyone we know. And for kids who are just learning how to speak, it's even more stressful and hurtful to be corrected, especially if there's an audience.

What should you do? How should you handle it when your child says "Me go park" when he wants to go to the park, or "More nana pwease" when she wants another banana? It's easier than you may think: Simply repeat the phrase correctly.

Here are a few examples of what we mean:

Child: Me go park.

Parent: Oh, you want to go back to the park?

Child: Uh-huh.

Parent: Yes, you do want to go to the park?

Child: Yeah.

Parent: Okay, well maybe we can go back to the park after naptime.

Child: More nana pwease.

Parent: Thank you for using such kind manners. I love hearing you say "please" when you ask for something. You would like some more banana?

Parent: Would you like blueberry jam or grape jam on your sandwich today?

Child: Boobewie.

Parent: You'd like blueberry jam on your sandwich? Great choice. One blueberry jam and cream cheese sandwich coming right up!

The more our kids hear us speaking correctly, the more likely our children will pick up on the natural cadences, syntax, and rhythm of our language.

Stop correcting. Just repeat correctly.

STORYTELLING ACTIVITIES BUILD ORAL LANGUAGE

Of all the benefits of encouraging your children to tell and share stories, the most amazing one is to connect them with their creativity. Young children may not be able to write yet, but writing is not the only way to create a story. Here are five easy tips you can use to get your young child involved in storytelling—without writing.

 ## TELL STORIES WITH PUPPETS.

You don't even need puppets—a few stuffed animals can be pulled into service to help your child create a story. If your child needs prompts to get started, suggest places for the puppets to go visit. Consider using places your child is familiar with, like the grocery store or library.

Choose one puppet or stuffed animal and ask your child to choose another. If your child is comfortable taking the lead and playing, just go with it. Do what you can to ask open-ended questions (questions that require more than a "yes" or "no" answer), and loosen up and get silly!

Consider using these prompts to get you started:

- ★ *Where should the animals travel today?*
- ★ *What will the animals do on a vacation?*
- ★ *Let's go to the store!*
- ★ *Let's go to the zoo!*

Remember,
these stories
don't have to
make a lot of
sense or be the
next bestseller.
They are
just fun little
ways to get
our kids using
new words
and thinking
creatively.

TELL POPCORN STORIES.

Popcorn stories are little stories that you tell using whatever pops into your head. Allison always starts with, "Once upon a time there was a ..." and then invites her preschooler to take over. When the story starts faltering, Allison steps back in with, "But then ..." and they continue to go back and forth, with Allison modeling for and supporting her daughter along the way.

If the story stalls while you're playing, try these transitions and connectors to keep it afloat:

- ★ And so ...
- ★ Because ...
- ★ Suddenly ...
- ★ Next ...

- ★ Before they ...
- ★ Meanwhile ...
- ★ However ...
- ★ And to their surprise ...

TELL YOUR OWN ADVENTURE STORIES.

Fight dragons. Save kittens from tall trees. Dive deep into the ocean to look for sunken treasure. The simple prompt of "What next?" has long helped us explore stories with young children by letting their imagination shine. Saying, "Let's spend some time telling stories" can be intimidating, but saying, "Let's go on an adventure" sounds *thrilling*.

A great way to start an adventure story is to make it all about your child. "There once was a prince named [your child's name], and one day he went on a fantastic adventure where he ..." Whenever your child is starting to stall, try, "What happened next?" Answering a question is a much easier task than making up a whole story.

TELL STORIES WITH STORYBOARDS.

A storyboard is basically a comic strip. Have your child draw pictures to tell you a story without words. There are no speech bubbles in this comic, just step-by-step drawings that illustrate the events from start to finish. We like using these after an event, such as a family vacation, holiday, or a milestone, like a birthday or first day of school. Your child could even use this as a way to share his or her day at school or daycare with you.

You don't need anything special—just a piece of paper with some defined boxes and something to draw with. With beginners, explain that stories are told in order of events and show them which box to start with and which to end with. Once the pictures are drawn, encourage your child to share the storyboard with other family members, retelling and embellishing the story. Ask questions to elicit more details—and to get your child using more language!

You can help kids get inspired by looking at the comics section of the newspaper or at a graphic novel. Or simply start by making your own storyboard and sharing it. Don't forget to read it out loud once it's complete!

TELL STORIES ABOUT FAMILY PHOTOS.

Young children don't always know how to get started when telling a story—many adults don't, either. One of our favorite ways to get children involved in storytelling is to use family photos as story prompts. You can use photo albums or scroll through photos on your phone or tablet. The goal here isn't really a cohesive story (although that is encouraged); the goal is for your child to start sharing details, and ultimately to go beyond what is obvious, getting into the story behind the picture.

As you flip through photos, use prompts like these to get your child talking:

★ *Where were we when this photo was taken? What were we doing?*

★ *What was the best part of this day?*

★ *Tell me about this picture.*

★ *How were you feeling in this picture?*

You will find that even if your child's answers are brief at the beginning, if you keep at it, they will get longer and more detailed. Soon your child will tell you more and more about the photos without prompts. What children are really doing is applying prior knowledge to create a story, and this is an important skill for learning.

Our favorite part of this simple activity is the connection that it creates between parent and child. It's priceless to hear a child's perspective of the events captured in family photos. Taking the time to listen to our children as they begin to learn to read will help build their trust in us as safe listeners. As children start reading, having someone they trust to read to and to listen to them is hugely important for building confidence. It is also an ideal opportunity for you to see how they are doing and to offer help if needed.

 USE SONGS TO EXPLORE LANGUAGE.

It's priceless to hear a child's perspective of the events captured in family photos.

Singing is an amazing tool for learning. Not only can you teach facts with song (Allison still sings the alphabet when putting anything in alphabetical order), you can help your child develop important literacy skills as well.

Many songs for young children include rhymes because they are fun and easy to remember. As children listen to and sing along with their favorites, they'll be developing their ability to hear and make rhymes, which is an essential skill for learning to read. Rhymes help children be able to eventually single out specific sounds in words and play with them, noticing how some words sound alike and some do not. When children can manipulate sounds like this, they will be able to recognize and create their own rhymes.

Often parents cringe when they think of music for kids, but children's music has come a long way. Today, many songs for children are sung by adult singers/songwriters, and the tunes are catchy and memorable for adults and kids alike.

Here are a few children's music albums with great sing-along songs that parents can sing with their children:

150 Toddler Tunes by Kidzup

The Singable Songs Collection by Raffi

One Elephant, Deux Éléphants by Sharon, Lois and Bram

Play some of this music in the car, at home, or in the playroom. It all counts!

Here Come the ABCs / Here Come the 123s by They Might Be Giants

The Best of the Laurie Berkner Band by Laurie Berkner Band

Kids in Motion by Greg & Steve

Songs in Spanish for Children by Martita, Jesus de Jerez & Juan Rojas

Lullaby by Jewel

Snacktime by Barenaked Ladies

Family Time by Ziggy Marley

Wee Sing Silly Songs by Pamela Conn Beall and Susan Hagen Nipp

TIP #18 WORK ON LISTENING SKILLS WITH SIMPLE TRICKS.

So much of developing oral language depends on good listening skills. We need children to hear new words, sounds within words, rhymes, and individual letter sounds as they get ready to read. Learning to listen well is so important that it's worth taking five minutes here and there as often as possible to work on it.

Here are a few tricks to use at home:

Use Play Phones

Next time your child pretends to talk on a phone, watch him or her carefully. Most children will imitate speaking as well as listening. Not only is this a great way to work on taking turns, but it's also a wonderful way to work on listening. Grab a play phone and get chatting!

You can make a phone out of a banana, a calculator (trust us, Amy's students do this daily), or use an old, deactivated cell phone to play "phone."

Need some conversation starters? Try these and see where they take you:

- ★ *What did you do today?*
- ★ *Let's go on an adventure today. Where should we go?*
- ★ *Where are you going after preschool?*
- ★ *What is your favorite book?*
- ★ *Please tell me what you would like to have for dinner.*
- ★ *I am at the grocery store but forgot my list. Can you tell me what I need to buy?*
- ★ *Pizza Palace. May I take your order?*

Take a Listening Walk

Listening Walks are our favorite calm activity to do with children.

Head out of the house and open your ears because as you walk, you are going to identify all the sounds you hear. Really. It's that simple, and it's a great way to connect with your child, too.

Depending on where you take your walk, the sounds you hear and share will obviously vary. Listening Walks are also a super time to build children's awareness of words. When you share your sounds, you'll be identifying both the sound and sound-maker.

Naming the sounds that you hear is a great way to expand that vocabulary a bit—*and* have a few laughs along the way. It's not about being 100% accurate in identifying the correct name of the sound or the sound-maker; it's about opening up your ears and really taking time to listen to the world around you.

Mealtime Telephone

Mealtime Telephone is simply when people pass a message from person to person via a whisper.

You can do it at home with as few as three people. The message may not get as garbled, but we can bet your children will still be trying their hardest to listen carefully, and that is what we want!

If you aren't familiar with this game, it's super simple. One person thinks of a short message and passes it along by whispering it to the next person. The last person in line announces it, and everyone can giggle at how the message changed along the way.

Here are some silly sentences to use for your own version of Mealtime Telephone:

- ★ *This supper is super!*
- ★ *This dinner is a winner.*
- ★ *Gobble up your grub, yum yum!*
- ★ *Kiss the cook and read a book!*

Listening Maps

This activity is similar to a Listening Walk, but you stay in one place.

Give your child a plain piece of paper, some colored pencils, and a clipboard. Go outside and find a comfy place to sit. Place the paper in front of your child and put an **x** to indicate where your child is on the map.

As you and your child sit quietly listening to the sounds around you, have your child write the sounds on the paper. If your neighbor is using the lawnmower, he or she would make an **x** (or other mark) and draw a lawnmower on the map in relation to him- or herself on the map.

Who knew this favorite childhood pastime had such great learning benefits?

This simple activity not only encourages children to stop and listen; it also teaches them mapping skills and encourages them to use their own creativity to draw the sounds they hear.

Vocabulary-Boosting Activities

When we read aloud to children, we have a captive audience—children hang on every word! Why not use this time to model how excited we are when we come across the use of rich and descriptive language?

By sharing our love of words and talking about new and exciting words, we are teaching our children to become word conscious, or word aware. We can do this by stopping during a read-aloud and commenting on a particularly awesome, unusual, or interesting word.

You can also help kids become word aware by:

- ★ Talking about the way a word sounds when you say it
- ★ Discussing the meaning of a new or unfamiliar word
- ★ Talking about the way a word looks on the page
- ★ Trying different ways of using a particular word
- ★ Challenging each other to use a new word later that day
- ★ Listening for new words during other read-alouds and taking turns "catching" them
- ★ Sharing new words as a family, at the end of the day or at dinnertime
- ★ Keeping a family list of "Cool New Words" or becoming "word wizards" and making a *Word Wizard Wall* of words you love

Developing word consciousness is easy, it's important, and it promotes a love of language and an awareness of words that will ultimately help strengthen reading comprehension down the road.

Word consciousness should start with our littlest learners and continue into adulthood.

TIP #19 FILL YOUR TOYBOX WITH VOCABULARY-BOOSTING TOYS.

The more a child talks with adults—or even older children—the more words he or she will use and hear. Talking helps children build vocabulary without even knowing it, so let's give them reasons to talk during play!

Think about including the following toys in your home:

★ puppets

★ toy microphones

★ play pianos

★ play phones

★ cash registers

★ dress-up clothes/costumes

★ magnifying glasses

★ binoculars

How can you use these toys to encourage kids to talk?

1. Dive into the dramatic! Use props as you role play, and talking will happen naturally.

2. Go on an adventure and talk about what you find.

3. Put on a talent show. (All you need is a clean bit of floor for a stage!)

4. Follow your child's lead and work in questions as they play. Questions don't have to be complicated or difficult. Just ask if you can play and see where it goes.

TIP #20

USE AN AT-HOME WORD BOARD.

If you have children in school, you've probably seen word walls before. Teachers post words they're teaching on the wall, organized alphabetically or by theme, so children can see them throughout the day and easily find them if they need them.

Words walls are a great place to showcase words your budding readers are learning. At home, you can size the word wall down to a whiteboard, and when your child encounters a new word, you can add it until it is learned and then move on to a new one. Not only will your child see these new words, they will be available for everyone in the house to talk about. The Word Board serves as a visual reminder for parents to weave these words into their daily conversation, offering the child more opportunity to hear the words being used correctly.

Here are some ideas for great categories of words to add to your Word Board:

- ★ seasonal words
- ★ weather words
- ★ color words
- ★ clothing words

These activities should be easy and fun because our goal in raising readers is to make the whole reading experience exciting.

★ family names

★ names of locations you have visited as a family

★ names of characters in books you are reading

Put the Word Board where your child can see it often; for example, near the breakfast table or even in your bathroom!

The goal is to use the board to spark interest in new words and to see the board often so that the words become familiar. If you want to get fancy, you can even write silly messages using the new word(s) on the board for your child to read.

 **CREATE A WORD JAR**

It will take you at most ten minutes to set up a Word Jar, but the benefits will be lasting. All you need is a jar (really any container will do), some strips of paper, and something to write with. Fill the jar with words your child isn't presently using, and you'll be amazed at how quickly the words start appearing in your child's everyday speech!

1. Make a list of words you want to introduce to your child. We like using words from books we are currently reading or have read recently, as this deepens the connection to books while giving children some context for the words.

2. Write the words on the strips of paper and pop them in the jar.

3. At a specified time (we like dinner), pull out a word and talk about it. Everyone at the table gets to make a guess at what the word means.

4. Choose one person to locate the definition of the word in a dictionary. Not only are you playing with words with this activity, you are also modeling how to use a dictionary.

Start simple, but as your children get good at being word detectives, make it tricky! Use a thesaurus to find antonyms and synonyms for everyday words, or randomly flip through a dictionary to find odd words even *you* aren't familiar with. Playing with words should be fun, and when you connect words to books that kids are reading, you will again be reinforcing the importance of books. And as you talk about the different words, you're also building your child's oral language. Way to go!

TIP #22 DEVELOP ORAL LANGUAGE: PLAY "ONE OF THESE THINGS"

Just like the old song "One of These Things Is Not Like the Other" from our *Sesame Street* days, this game is an oldie but a goodie.

You can play this game with just about anything in your house, and the concept is super simple: Choose several items that are similar and one that is different, then challenge your child to pick the one that doesn't belong. Simply say to your child, *One of these things is not like the others. Think hard for a minute or two, then tell me which one is not like the others.*

When your child identifies the object that's not like the other, ask him or her to tell you why. The second part is where you get your child thinking, talking, and explaining.

With this activity, kids are thinking, categorizing, and speaking—all skills integral for word learning and reading!

Keep in mind that for younger children you'll want to use a smaller number of objects, about two or three, that are the same and one that is different; as kids get older, you can add more.

Here are a few ideas for objects:

★ clothing: socks and a shirt; pants and a shoe; mittens and a hat; etc.

★ food: apples and an orange; raisins and a grape; dry noodles and cooked noodles; etc.

★ household items: utensils and a bowl; toothbrushes and toothpaste; pens and paper; etc.

★ outdoor items: rocks and a leaf; grass and dirt; flower petals and a weed; etc.

 **CREATE A SENSORY BOX.**

Get kids touching and smelling and listening—and then talking!

First, let's cover the basics: What is a sensory box and why do I want to let my child play with one? At its most basic, a sensory box is a plastic container filled with some kind of substance, such as dry rice. However, in most sensory boxes, you will find tools for scooping whatever filling is being used, small toys or figurines to manipulate, and other objects to discover. Children certainly explore textures with their hands, but the most wonderful thing that happens with these simple tools is that children talk, tell stories, and connect with language. The other literacy benefit to these sometimes messy boxes are the opportunities for children to work on developing their fine-motor skills. They will need strong fine-motor skills when they begin writing.

How do you make a sensory box? For an at-home sensory box, we suggest a shallow plastic bin with a lid. This lets you store the box without taking it all apart, and at the same time keeps bugs (or your unsupervised child) out.

In addition to a plastic bin, you need filler. Consider using:

- ★ dry rice
- ★ dry pasta
- ★ dry beans* or lentils
- ★ unpopped popcorn
- ★ cracked corn
- ★ flax seeds
- ★ oats

- ★ birdseed
- ★ small pebbles
- ★ beads
- ★ plastic or paper "grass"
- ★ pom-poms
- ★ cotton balls

Next you need some fun things to pop in the sensory box with the filler. Here are some of our favorites:

- ★ smaller containers
- ★ scoops
- ★ little figurines
- ★ blocks
- ★ marbles

- ★ chunky puzzle pieces
- ★ construction vehicles
- ★ bits of nature, such as sticks, leaves, and/or bigger rocks

* Skip kidney beans as they can be toxic if ingested while raw.

Now what do you *do* with it? When playing with a sensory box, participate with your child. Model how to keep the filler in the box, and strike up a conversation. You don't have to purposefully introduce new words or start telling stories; just try to look at things from your child's perspective. Narrate what you are doing and ask open-ended questions to encourage him or her to join in the conversation.

Here are some things Allison says when using the sensory box in her classroom:

★ *Wow, this rice feels nice on my hands!*

★ *I wonder if I can fill this container all the way up to the top?*

★ *How many of these figurines are there in the box?*

★ *I like this color. Which color in the sensory box do you like best?*

★ *I like the sound the corn makes while I pour it.*

Use all of the senses (well, maybe not taste) with these boxes to ignite as many new experiences as you can.

From telling stories to exploring word meanings, the richer the language your child hears from you, the more likely you'll hear this language coming from your child.

IT'S ALL ABOUT THE BOOK

Let's get book-happy.

Concepts of print. Print awareness. Sounds totally big-time, but it's really not. It's just about showing your child what to do with books when he or she is holding one, and generally what readers do when they're looking at print on a page, in the environment, anywhere.

Most of us are so comfortable with books that we don't give print concepts a second thought. However, teaching our children about the *concepts of print* when reading aloud is one of those simple things we can do that packs a powerful punch.

Take five minutes here and there to demonstrate these simple skills, and your little one will be well on the way to handling books like a pro!

Concepts of print include knowing how to:

★ Identify the front and back covers of the book

★ Point out the name of the book, author, and illustrator

★ Show where to begin reading on a page

★ Follow the left-right direction of words and the return sweep of print

★ "Read" punctuation marks

★ Notice differences in print—boldface, italics, underlining, font size, and so on

★ Point out captions of photographs

★ Look at labels and diagrams

 TIP #24 **LET YOUR CHILD TEACH YOU HOW TO USE A BOOK.**

Children learn how books work long before they learn how to read. You will see babies flipping through books, turning them over if they open them upside down, and looking at the pages left to right, front to back. We aren't born knowing these things; we learn by watching as our parents and other adults read to us. That's why it's important to read aloud to your child early and often.

Your little one will pick up so much just by watching you!

One of the things we like doing with kids is pretending to be an alien from outer space who has never seen a book before. We get really silly flipping the book around pretending not to know how to open it, asking what the names on the cover are for, what the title is, and so on. Children will always pipe up and teach us. Then we try to read from the back to the front, flipping pages at random and looking at the pictures upside down.

The giggles are plentiful. The learning is, too. Children love being the teacher. This silly little activity is short enough to do at bedtime or even in a waiting room. It's effective. It reinforces what children do know and might even create an opportunity to teach them something new.

TIP #25 HAVE A LIBRARY-BOOK PARADE.

Nothing will get a child to focus on the covers of books like a library-book parade! We're not talking about a parade with bands and floats and gymnastics teams. We're talking about an easy, quiet, at-home parade so each of those great books you brought home from the library has a chance to really shine! It's a print-concept party at its most basic.

Let your child get a really good look at the books you borrowed from the library simply by putting the books "on parade" on a table, shelf, or dresser in your home. All you need to do is have your child nearby as you pull a book out of your bag and read aloud the title, author, and illustrator. Then set the book up on display, where your child can readily see it, and do the same thing for the next book.

The parade can be as long or as short as you'd like—just make sure it's long enough for each book to have some time in the spotlight!

Consider encouraging your child to group the books, sorting them in any way he or she sees fit. Think about putting on a book parade every few days, with the books you already have at home—it's a great way to revive oldies-but-goodies and move books from room to room!

GO ON A BOOK WALK.

Not as in-depth as a read-aloud but not as quick as a skim, "a book walk" is a great way for kids to practice retelling a familiar story.

A book walk is a "walk" through the book, in which your child tells the story in his or her very own words, starting at the beginning. Using the pictures and words your child recognizes on the page as a guide, a book walk is a great, quick strategy to help your little one practice speaking, listening, and retelling.

Choose a familiar book and:

★ Ask your child to take you on a book walk because he or she knows the book so well and you'd like to hear the story again.

★ Use a book walk when there's not enough time to read the whole book word for word.

★ Have your child take a sibling on a book walk while you answer an email, put away groceries, etc. (But really listen and watch the whole time!)

Not only do book walks let little ones practice their speaking and thinking skills, but they also give kids a chance to show that they understand basic concepts of print, such as opening the book, pointing out words they may recognize, and moving through the book from start to finish.

TIP #27 PLAY GRID GAMES.

Grid games seem super-easy, but they're powerful tools for helping kids learn basic concepts of print. The process of moving deliberately from left to right, object-by-object, and line-by-line will help kids learn the left-right-return-sweep movement of reading! The more we can replicate that very simple movement—left to right and back again—the better.

At their most basic, grid games consist of a sheet of paper with pictures or shapes laid out in a symmetrical, orderly fashion. Grid games geared toward younger kids might have three rows of 5 items each, while grid games for older kids could have five rows of 8 to 10 items each (see image at right).

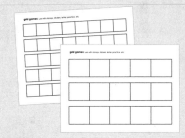

Playing a grid game, no matter what size grid you use, is simple.

Download grid templates from our websites: teachmama.com and notimeforflashcards.com.

You need:

- ★ grid game sheets (one for each player)
- ★ tokens or markers, one to cover each item (consider using dried beans, o-cereal bits, or pennies)
- ★ a die or pack of cards (use only numbers 2–6) to determine number

To play:

1. Decide together who will go first.
2. Player One rolls a die or flips a card.

3. Player One covers the number of items that he/she flipped or rolled, starting with the object in the far left square and moving to the right.

4. Player Two follows steps 2 to 3. Players continue taking turns.

5. The winner is the person who covers his or her grid sheet first!

Extremely simple, yes, but kids are learning important skills while playing.

MAKE SURE YOUR CHILD KNOWS THAT EVERY WORD ON A PAGE MATCHES A WORD BEING READ ALOUD.

Every letter and *every* word count in reading, and you can help your child understand this by practicing one-to-one correspondence in fun and easy ways.

One-to-one correspondence is commonly associated with math, but it's also an important element in early literacy education. One-to-one correspondence can be pointing to each item in a group as you count them; for instance, placing one cracker at a time on a plate as you count up to the number allotted for today's snack. In reading, we want early readers to point to each word as they say it. We can model this by pointing to each word we read on a page.

Other fun and simple ways to teach kids this concept are to:

★ Touch each finger or toe as you count it
★ Place one object in each section of an egg carton, muffin tin, or ice-cube tray
★ Count the cars as they drive by your house
★ Touch each rock on your front stoop

When you're reading a book with your child, try doing the following things to reinforce one-to-one correspondence as you point to each word:

★ Use a feather to follow each word as it's read

★ Put on a plastic finger to point to each word as it's read

★ Make and use silly pointers using a craft stick with an eyeball on the top, a straw with a gold star stapled to the top, or tiny finger puppets made from baby-sized socks

★ Use clean and dry bubble wands to create a pointer that also circles each word as it's read

No matter what you choose to point with, teaching this important concept can be simple but really fun.

Understanding how books work and how to follow the print on a page are key concepts that don't come naturally to children, so the five minutes here and there you spend demonstrating them will really pay off!

SOUND CHECK: PLAYING WITH SOUNDS

Sound check. Is this mic on?

It only takes five minutes here and there to help your child pick up on those teeny-tiny, über-important sounds.

Phonological awareness is a fancy name for hearing and identifying individual sounds in words—like *alliteration* (the repeated beginning sound in a series of words) or *rhyme* (the repeated middle or end sounds of words).

Rhyme is a simple and natural way for children to begin "playing" with word sounds. And because often rhyme can be silly (think: *the fat cat sat on a mat*), rhyme also helps children begin to see the fun in language learning. This is our goal, friends. We always want to emphasize the fun so that kids know how entertaining and cool learning can be!

We begin to identify beginning and ending word sounds since they are the easiest for kids to hear. Beginning sound play can be as simple as saying, "Look at the items here on the table. I see a cup, a car, and a sock. *Cup, car, sock*. I can hear that two of these things start with the same sound. Can you hear it, too? *Cup, car, sock*. Which two of these things start with the same beginning sound? Yes, you can hear it—*cup* and *car* do begin with the same sound: /k/!"

Ultimately, we want children to be able to hear *each* individual sound in a word. So for the word *cat*, we want them to be able to hear three sounds: /k/, /a/, and /t/—which is easier said than done! We first begin by helping kids hear syllables in words, you remember—"clapping out the words." This is the first step in breaking words down into their smaller sound units.

Eventually we want kids to hear *all* the sounds in a word—even the tricky middle ones. And more than that, we want them to be able to *play* with those sounds, to be able to take out a sound and substitute a different one, so they can go from *cat* to *at* to *bat*. Teacher-talk for this word play is "manipulating" sound, but we prefer "playing with"—and it really is fun for little ones! Whatever you call it, it's a really big deal. In fact, it's so important that if children don't get it, they won't get reading. So let's get on the phonological awareness stuff, stat!

> Rhyming is hugely helpful for helping kids learn to distinguish sounds in words. And rhyming is fun, which makes it a natural motivator for building vocabulary.

TIP #29   MAKE A RHYME, ANYTIME.

You're probably a poet and you don't even know it.

Share your skills with your kids. You'll be so incredibly glad you did.

Here are a few rhyming games to play anywhere, any time. These activities work best when you have a group of kids or the whole family involved.

> **Rhyme Challenge:** Start with a word, like *cat*, and each person adds a word that rhymes until you run out of words.

Crazy Animal Rhyme: Begin with something simple, like *fat cat*, and follow the pattern of a rhyming adjective (describing word) + an animal until everyone's laughing too hard to speak clearly. Don't worry—there's no "wrong" here. Some ideas: *shakey snakey, squishy fishy, foul owl.*

Speed Rhyme Pairs: One person begins by sharing a word, and another person shouts out a word that rhymes with it, making a rhyme pair. Immediately after calling out the rhyme pair, that person calls out a new word. Then, a third person shouts a rhyme pair for that word, and so on. Lots of laughs. Lots of noise.

Timed Rhyme: Everyone is given the same word and one minute to write down as many rhyming words as they can. Whoever gets the most rhymes wins! This game is also a cool way of incorporating writing and counting into a rhyme game.

So much of your kids' excitement over something as simple as listening for sounds in words hinges on how *you* feel about sounds in words. So ham it up. Make rhyme the most awesome thing you ever knew, even just for a few minutes each day. We guarantee that if you do, your kids will soon develop an "ear" for sounds, too.

TIP #30 — PLAY THE NAME GAME TO PRACTICE SOUNDS.

Having fun with letter sounds is easier than you think. You may have even played some of these games already with your children and didn't even stop to think that you were teaching them as you played!

Making the game personal is a really powerful element here; doing so creates a deeper-level connection with the concepts and, therefore, a deeper level of learning.

This is a great game for after dinner or while waiting at a restaurant.

The Name Game is a simple language game that uses a child's first name to start, then branches out from there.

To play:

1.   Player One says the first letter of his or her first name followed by "*my name is* [insert name], *and I come from* [place that starts with the same letter], *and I like* [insert item that starts with the letter]."

2.   Have each player take a turn. After the first round, move to your middle names, and finally your last.

For example Allison would say: "A, my name is Allison. I come from Alberta, and I like avocados."

If the next person were named Jason he might say, "*J*, my name is Jason. I come from Jacksonville, and I like jellybeans!"

You can make the game more challenging by encouraging your child to name as many items as possible that start with the target letter. For example, "A, my name is Allison. I come from Alberta, and I like apples, avocados, ants, art . . ."

Another way to make the game more challenging is to simply work through the whole alphabet from A to Z. If your child gets stuck, you can offer a little help. If you are playing with several children, encourage players to help each other out. This isn't a win-or-lose game; it's a challenge to tackle together! As your child plays, he or she will be developing knowledge of letter sounds as well as learning about geography and building vocabulary. Since this game requires no materials, it's a perfect game to play anywhere. It's one of our family's favorite road trip games.

MAKE A RHYMING TREASURE BOX.

Rhyming isn't just important for future poets and rappers—it's an important literacy skill that helps children play with and recognize patterns in words. Plain and simple, when children rhyme, they are strengthening their phonological awareness and building a more solid foundation for learning to read. We want them to have as strong a foundation as possible.

Set-up

For this activity, you will need a handful of small toys, some small squares of paper, a pencil, and a basket for the toys. Write out words on the sheets of paper that rhyme with the names of the toys you have gathered.

To play:

1. Have your little rhymer choose a piece of paper.

2. Read it together. Modeling reading is important and doesn't have to be saved only for read-alouds.

3. Find the toy from the basket that rhymes with the word.

4. Keep going until the basket is empty.

Next Steps

Once your child has mastered this activity, you can omit the pieces of paper and have him choose a toy, then come up with a rhyming word on his own. You can also play with multiple players, each one taking turns drawing toys from the basket. Each toy rhyme equals one point. If a player can't come up with a rhyme, the toy returns to the basket. The player with the most points wins.

TIP #32 PLAY RHYME BINGO.

Any form of bingo is a win for kids. Add a little rhyme, and it's a major score.

Rhyme Bingo requires only a few things: Rhyme Bingo cards, Rhyme Bingo boards, and items to use as bingo markers, like pennies or buttons.

Rhyme Bingo rocks because our version can be played even before kids can read, since the boards have pictures instead of words.

Download bingo cards and bingo boards from our websites, teachmama.com and notimeforflashcards.com

To play:

1. Download and print the Rhyme Bingo boards and cards from our websites (see box at right).

2. Take a minute to name all of the pictures on the cards.

3. Then, give each player a Rhyme Bingo board and bingo markers.

4. Shuffle all of the cards and place them facedown in a pile between the boards.

5. Flip the top card and say the name of the picture.

6. Players check their bingo cards to see if they have a picture on their card that rhymes with the name of that picture.

7. Show your child how to check for a rhyme match. Hold the card next to each picture as you go from left to right across the rows, saying the word of the picture you flipped and the word pictured in each box, listening to the similarities or differences between the sounds.

8. If a player finds a match, he or she places a bingo marker on that square.

9. Repeat Steps 5 and 6. The winner is the player who gets bingo (three in a row).

TIP #33

PLAY RHYMING GO FISH.

Kids dig any form of Go Fish! Try throwing some rhyme into the pond, and they'll flip for it.

Download Go Fish cards from our websites, teachmama.com and notimeforflashcards.com.

All you need to play Rhyming Go Fish are rhyming picture cards. That's it. You can use the same picture cards as you did for Rhyme Bingo (available on our websites) or you can make your own from pictures cut out of magazines. You and your child can play this game together, but it works best with three or more players.

The premise of any Go Fish game is to be the person who gets the most pairs. In Rhyming Go Fish, the focus is rhyming pairs, so players try to get two picture cards that rhyme.

To play:

1. Mix up all of the cards and deal each player five cards. Place the remaining cards facedown in the "pond" in the middle of the table.

2. Players match any rhyming pairs in their hand and lay them down, then take cards from the pond so that each player begins with five cards.

3. Player One asks Player Two, "*Do you have a card with a picture that rhymes with* [word on card]?"

4. If Player Two has a rhyming card, he says "*Yes, I do. Here's* [rhyming word]," and hands Player One the card. If Player Two does not have a rhyming card, he says, "*Nope. Go, fish!*"

5. Player One then "fishes" for the card in the pond. If Player One gets a card that rhymes with the selected card, then she says, "*I fished my wish!*" and lays down the pair. If not, the new card is simply added to the player's hand.

6. Now it becomes Player Two's turn, starting at Step 3. The game ends when all of a player's cards are laid-down pairs. The winner is the player with the most pairs.

At the end of the game, just to make sure your child is hearing rhyme sounds as often as possible (and to double-check all rhymes), have him or her say all of the rhyme pairs out loud. The more our kids can hear and say rhyming sounds, the better.

TIP #34

CLAP OUT THOSE SYLLABLES.

You may remember counting syllables or clapping syllables back in grade school. That was really important stuff! Syllables are like beats in music, except syllables are sounds in words. For example, the word *pepper* consists of two syllables — /pep/ + /er/ — while *television* has four: /tel/ + /e/ + /vizh/ + /un/. The easiest way to identify syllables is by clapping words—each clap representing one syllable.

You can practice this important skill anywhere, any time. You can start by saying:

★ *Did you know that words have beats, just like music?*

★ *The beats in words are called "syllables."*

★ *Listen as I clap out the beats in my name:* Mom-my [clap, clap]

★ *Which has more syllables: Madeline or Cora?* [*Ma-de-line,* clap, clap, clap; *Co-ra,* clap, clap]

★ *Let's try to clap out the syllables in all of our friends'/ family members'/ pets' names.*

★ *Can you think of three names with one syllable?*

★ *I wonder if we can think of a name with four or five syllables?*

As your child becomes familiar with the process of breaking words into sounds, you can play with any words you like! Ask your child to compare two or three words and tell which one has the most or least syllables, then challenge your child to come up with a word in a category that has a certain number of syllables, such as: *Can you think of a color word that has three syllables in it? (indigo, magenta,* etc.). This can be a great way to build vocabulary too!

Why spend time on syllables? When kids can hear and identify groups of sounds in words, they're more likely to break apart words and identify specific sounds within them. Isolating individual sounds will ultimately help children both in writing words and in decoding (reading) words.

Woot!

TIP #35 CLAP OUT FAMILY NAMES AND WIN!

Syllable segmentation sounds pretty serious, but the skill is just breaking down words into sounds. It's important to practice this skill with your child because when he or she can recognize and break down words into sounds, it's much easier to decode (read!) words. Here's a fun way to practice with family names. Grab a pencil, paper (or index cards), and some scissors (although we usually just rip ours). Write out family names on individual pieces of paper. Use long names, short nicknames, and names that are in between. We use our extended family and even our pets' names—they are part of the family, right?

Shuffle the cards and place them on the table.

Make sure that you have enough cards for everyone to have the same number of turns. We usually do three rounds of the game. For a family of four that means making 12 cards.

A fun way to work on syllables at home is to turn them into a game for the whole family.

To play:

1. Each player takes a turn picking a card and breaking down the name on the card by clapping out the syllables.

2. Players get one point per syllable.

3. At the end of the game, the player with the most points wins.

SORT SOUNDS.

If kids can hear the individual sounds in words, they're off to a seriously strong start.

As we all know, sorting is simply the act of organizing objects into specific groups. Just like we sort our laundry into darks, lights, and whites or our coupons into baking, dairy, and personal in our little coupon organizer, sorting is a crazy-important skill for children to practice as their brains develop. Sorting is used in all kinds of ways in school and in life, so it's a great skill to practice early and often!

Sorting activities can, and should, start at a young age. And sorting should be practiced with a lot of modeling, which means you lead the way by showing how it's done and talking about what you're doing and why (which is building those oral language skills too—two for one!). For early sorting activities, you might say: *Let's put all of the blocks in the blue bin and all of the doll clothes in the red bin.* Or, *Can you help me put the markers, crayons, and colored pencils into these three containers?*

> Sorting is used in all kinds of ways in school and in life.

These directed sorts will pave the way for more open-ended sorts, where your child uses his or her own ideas to determine how things should be sorted. When your child is ready, you can leave the organization up to him or her: *We have all of these art supplies in the box, and it's hard to find what we need. How can we use these three containers to make them more organized?*

All this early practice sorting objects will help children build a foundation for a clear understanding of the concept of sorting when it comes to the more abstract idea of sorting words by their sounds. A great place to begin is at the beginning, of course—beginning sounds of words, that is! Since the focus here is on sounds and not letters, this sort uses pictures or actual objects. Read on for details.

Making a Beginning-Sound Sort:

1. Grab about 8 to 12 pictures or small toys. You can tear pages out of magazines, glue small photos on index cards, or print out the sorting cards available on our websites (teachmama.com and notimeforflashcards.com). If possible, find a mix of objects that begin with two or three very different sounds: such as /m/ (moon, money, Mom) or /s/ (snake, sea, sun) or /t/ (tree, train, turtle).

2. Say the name of each picture as you go through them one by one.

3. Place the cards face up so that you can see all of them.

4. Explain that you are going to work together to put these pictures into groups. Share that you will both really need strong ears because you're going to sort these pictures according to their beginning sounds. You are going to try to find the words that begin with the same sound as moon, snake, and tree.

5. Place those three pictures in a row, saying each word as you put it on the table. These are your "anchor words."

6. Now it's time to sort! Pick up another card and say the word, emphasizing the beginning sound. Say, Money. Mmmmmoney. I hear the M sound at the beginning of money, so let's see where it belongs. Does money have the same beginning sound as moon? Mmmmoney, mmmmoon. Or does it have the same beginning sound as snake? Mmmmmoney, ssssssnake. One last word to check.

Let's see if it has the same beginning sound as tree. *Mmmmmoney, tttttttree. Okay, what do you think?*

7. *Yes!* Money *has the same beginning sound as* moon, *so we put the card here, under the moon card. Let's do the next one.*

Something to note: The direct comparison of sounds while holding the cards next to each other is very helpful for teaching children to develop an ear for sounds. Even if your child can make the call immediately that *money* has the same beginning sound as *moon*, take the time to walk through the other sounds so he or she can hear the differences.

It doesn't matter whether you're working on beginning, middle, or ending sounds. Taking the short bit of time to make each comparison will help. For example, when working with *-at* family rhyme sounds, you might say: *We're listening for the –at sound in our rhyme cards today.* Cat, hat. Cat, hat. *I hear the –at sound in both of those words, do you?* Cat, hat. *Let's look at the next picture. It's a pot.* Cat, pot, Cat, pot. *Let's look at them all:* cat, hat, pot. Cat, hat, pot. *Which word doesn't sound the same as* cat—hat *or* pot?

Clapping, sorting, rhyming, matching—we told you phonological awareness could be fun! Work these short, fun activities into your repertoire and your child will have a solid foundation for learning to read.

LEARN. THOSE. LETTERS!

A, B, C, D, EFG, H, I, J, K, LMNOP. . .

Okay, you know your child should know the letters of the alphabet, but how on earth do we teach them, save from singing the "ABC Song" over and over and over? And even with singing, your child is only saying the letters—not seeing them.

So? You got this.

You totally do.

Five minutes here and there, and your child will know the letters of the alphabet. Done.

TIP #37 LET YOUR CHILD'S INTEREST TAKE THE LEAD WHEN TEACHING THE ALPHABET.

We get asked all the time: "What letter should I start with when I am introducing letters to my child? Uppercase or lowercase?"

Our best answer is: "Start with your child."

Let us explain what we mean.

The most important part of learning letters is to know the sounds they make, but *letter recognition* is the other piece of the letter puzzle. In early childhood education circles, there is a lot of debate about whether to start with uppercase letters, lowercase letters, or do them in tandem.

As teachers, we've noticed that when students come to us, most of them have a stronger grasp of uppercase letters, and as parents we've noticed how many alphabet-related toys and books use uppercase letters while omitting the lowercase ones. An important point is that uppercase letters are easier to identify; their shapes are more distinct and easier for kids to write.

Those are the arguments for the uppercase-first camp, but the lowercase-first camp's best argument is that when children are learning to read, the texts are not written in all uppercase. Rather, the majority of letters they will read will be lowercase.

We personally think both camps have valid points, so we teach our own children the letters in tandem. Like our students, our children learned their uppercase letters quickly, with the use of books and toys geared toward toddlers. We then focused on matching activities where our children could match upper- and lowercase letters. Children will pick up some letter recognition from their environment, like signs, toys, or even TV shows. Our advice is to start with your child and decide on a formal approach based on his or her interests.

Whether you start with upper- or lowercase letters, you should start with the letters in your child's name, beginning with the first letter of the first name. Nothing is more meaningful in print than one's own name, so it's a great place to start formal letter identification. Then you can move on to the names of family members, friends, and pets. You'll be amazed at how well kids associate letters with the names of familiar people! When new facts, concepts, and ideas are paired with experience, the information usually sticks, so you can also use your child's favorite things to help teach letters—dinosaur names, ballet steps, art supplies—whatever your child loves.

TIP #38 TEACH UPPER- AND LOWERCASE LETTERS WITH MATCHING GAMES.

Once children have started showing a real interest in letters and can identify them (upper- or lowercase, whichever they've learned first), the next step is to teach them that each letter comes in more than one shape. We stay away from saying "big" and "little" because you can write a lowercase letter on a huge piece of paper and call it "big." You can also write a teeny tiny uppercase letter and describe it as "little."

Instead, use the proper terms when speaking about letters, calling them "uppercase" and "lowercase." Here are two simple games to play that match upper- and lowercase letters.

A fun way to drive home the idea that upper- and lowercase letters are different forms of the same letter is to play matching games.

Before you play, make simple alphabet cards with cardstock and a permanent marker. Cut out 52 squares and write out the alphabet twice, once in lowercase letters and once in uppercase letters. You can laminate them to make them last longer.

Memory Match

Pick 10 to 12 letters, putting both the upper- and lowercase versions into the pile. Shuffle and place the cards facedown on a table. Take turns flipping cards to find matches. As your child masters this game, put in trickier letters. The letters *b*, *d*, *q*, and *p* are the ones children tend to struggle with the most. That said, follow your child's lead and balance success with challenge.

Go Fish!

Use all the cards for this game. Deal out five cards each and play. Play as you would a traditional Go Fish game, "fishing" for letters instead of numbers. (See detailed rules under Rhyming Go Fish on page 61.) The first person with no cards in his or her hand wins. It is important to encourage your child to use the proper terminology by modeling it yourself:

★ *Do you have an uppercase* T? or

★ *No, I do not have a lowercase* g.

If you use the correct terminology, your child will follow suit.

TIP #39
USE ALPHABET PUZZLES TO WORK ON LETTER RECOGNITION.

Although there are just 26 letters in the English alphabet, children have to learn both upper- and lowercase letters to be functional readers. They also have to be able to recognize all letters in different fonts, handwriting, sizes, shapes, and colors—you get the point.

It's more than just 26 letters.

These two simple puzzle games and their fun adaptations are great ways to work on letter identification, and the games won't take more than ten minutes to set up.

Index Card Match-up

Using index cards, write an uppercase letter on the left and its lowercase version on the right. Cut down the middle with scissors. Don't just cut a straight line; make squiggles, jagged edges, and waves, like a jigsaw puzzle.

Pop these pieces in a plastic bag that you can take along with you for waits at the dentist or doctor's office, airport, or to an older sibling's sporting event. It's easy—and it is self-checking! Your child will know she's found a match when the pieces fit together.

Find and Fit

This is a great activity for children who love—no, NEED—to move. (In case you aren't sure if that applies to your child, we can assure you it applies to almost every child!)

Incorporating movement adds fun and much-needed energy burn to a plain letter-match game.

Use the index card pieces from Index Card Match-up (page 71) and hide the lowercase letters around your home. Send your child to search for them. When a piece is found, have your child fit it together with its uppercase ones. The hunt is over when all pairs have been matched.

 TIP #40 READ ALPHABET BOOKS TO REINFORCE LETTER RECOGNITION.

We love the alphabet—but there's a lot to learn about each of those 26 letters! Children need to know what sounds a letter makes and what it looks like so they can make the right sound when they see it. What's brilliant about alphabet books is that because the pages are in alphabetical order, children can also feel a real sense of accomplishment when they know the next letter as the page is turned.

This sense of order gives kids the confidence to work on the harder things, like letter sounds and identification—they know the order because of the alphabet song, but don't necessarily connect the letter they are singing with the letter's shape. In addition, alphabet books give children exposure to less common words that they might not get a chance to encounter regularly in other books or in everyday life, such as *iguana* for *i*, *trombone* for *t*, or *gabon* for *g*. And these "exotic" words come with pictures too! Alphabet books are one of our favorite ways to work on letters with children when we only have a few minutes.

We encourage you to find books that include both upper- and lowercase letters in their pages, but the most important thing to look for is a book that your child will enjoy. Here are six fantastic alphabet books to enjoy and learn with:

1. **Animalia** by Graeme Base
   This picture book is filled to the gills with images of objects that start with each letter. Great for letter sounds.

2. **Eating the Alphabet** by Lois Elhert
   Food is something all kids can relate to, and this book uses both upper- and lowercase letters to introduce new foods and letter sounds to readers.

3. **Chicka Chicka Boom Boom** by Bill Martin Jr. and John Archambault
   A great kid-friendly beat will have you and your child singing, and the mix of upper- and lowercase letters is perfect for young learners.

4. **Superhero ABC** by Bob McLeod
   One by one, each letter is introduced with its own superhero and an alliterative description that will get your child laughing (and wanting to learn the letters!).

5. **Alphabet Under Construction** by Denise Fleming
   This book focuses on uppercase letters but couples them perfectly with action words that help reinforce letter sounds.

6. **The Sleepy Little Alphabet: A Bedtime Story From Alphabet Town** by Judy Sierra
   This is a great book for children learning to match, or having trouble connecting, upper- and lowercase letters. The uppercase letters tuck their corresponding lowercase letters to bed in this cute bedtime story.

PLAY I SPY THE LETTER . . .

The goal here is to open our children's eyes to the fact that letters are everywhere—all around them—and that once they learn the letters and can read words, they will find messages everywhere.

Get them into the habit of searching high and low for individual letters of the alphabet, and you may be surprised at how sharp your little ones' eyes are. As you find each letter, talk about its shape, style, and size: *Does it look like a typical letter? Was it easy to spy? What is unique about this letter? Does it look unusual because it's on a sign or logo?*

To add a bit of a challenge, encourage your child to:

★ Be the first one to find five *A*'s in the grocery store

★ Find the most beautiful letter *B* on a road sign

★ Locate the smallest letter *C* on the menu at a restaurant

★ Search for a stick in the shape of a letter

★ Find a letter *S* on the soccer field

Finding letters anywhere and everywhere opens the door to conversations about some really cool topics, such as letter sounds, fonts, uppercase and lowercase letters, and so on.

There's nothing like natural, on-the-spot learning like this. So start searching!

TIP #42 GO ON AN ALPHABET HUNT.

The idea here is to present children with the entire alphabet—it can simply be handwritten on paper—and then have them hunt for each letter. The goal is to find every single letter of the alphabet!

Letter learning can—and should—happen as often as possible. When kids are busy working hard at being Alphabet Hunters, long waits at the doctor's office or in traffic jams seem much shorter than they really are.

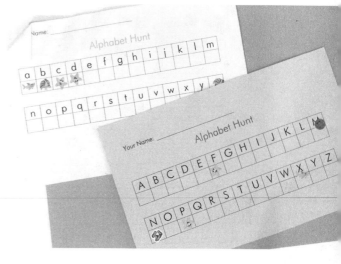

The cool thing is that an alphabet hunt can be done just about anywhere or anytime, with just about any supplies you have on hand. If you set up the alphabet hunt as an adventure with your child as an explorer, the possibilities are endless.

For an alphabet hunt, you always want to play with the entire alphabet, regardless of whether your child knows all of the letters or not. Our goal is to set our kids up for success, so if your child is already able to correctly identify some letters, then this activity will help to reinforce that knowledge as he or she works on new letters.

Write down the letters of the alphabet on a piece of paper and as you and your child find letters—in magazines, on signs or menus, or in any print in view—have him or her:

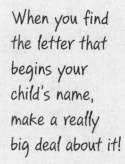

When you find the letter that begins your child's name, make a really big deal about it!

- ★ Use a marker to put an X next to each letter
- ★ Stick a small sticker next to each letter
- ★ Highlight letters
- ★ Circle each letter

Kids often follow their parents' lead in terms of energy level and enthusiasm when it comes to these kinds of activities, so the more excited you are when you find a letter, the better.

USE MEALTIME FOR LETTER HUNTING.

As a child, Amy vividly recalls arguing with her sisters over who would "get" certain cereal boxes at breakfast time. Getting the box meant it sat squarely in front of you so you could stare at it while you shoved cereal in your mouth.

Little did she realize how important the letters and words on those boxes were until she was a parent and was leaning on those boxes to help her own children learn the letters of the alphabet!

So what we're saying is, don't worry about being quick to put away the cereal boxes during breakfast. And if you don't do cold cereal in the morning, consider investing in some placemats for your kids to use at mealtime. Not only will the placemats help keep crumbs in one spot (or so we hope), they also are guaranteed reading material.

You can find great quality placemats complete with letters, numbers, shapes, or colors on them, or you can get crafty and make your own. All you need to whip up some homemade placemats are two pieces of construction paper, markers, glue or tape, stickers, magazines (for cutting out photos, letters, or words), and some clear contact paper.

To make a placemat:

1. Glue or tape the two edges of construction paper together so that the total placemat length is about 16″ long and 11″ high.

2. Decorate! Use anything and everything you can to make the design fun and engaging.

3. Cover the placemat in clear contact paper so that food and water will easily wipe away.

Mealtime letter hunting is simple and easy. Sure, it's similar to the letter hunting you can do out and about, but it's nearby and concentrated. Why not capitalize on that teeny bit of time for some fun learning?

When it comes down to the actual letter hunting, what should you say? How can you, as a tired and worn-out parent, make hunting for letters fun for your kids? It's all in the delivery.

Say something like:

★ *Ooooooh, I like what I see! I can see YOUR letter on this cereal box! Can you see it? Lucky letter C is right there in front of me!*

★ *Wow, there are a ton of letters looking at me this morning. I see an uppercase O and an uppercase M and . . . oh my! I see a lowercase y right over there. Can you point to a letter O or M?*

★ *Look at this! I love the way that this letter K is written with the dark green and blue sparkle. Follow with your finger as I do, like we're writing the K on the box.*

★ *Would you do me a favor while you're eating your breakfast and tell me three letters that are peeking out at you from that placemat?*

★ *Get out of town! Can you believe it? There are FIVE letter L's on the side of this box! I see three uppercase L's and two lowercase l's. Oh my goodness!*

With 26 letters of the alphabet to know and remember, letter learning will not happen overnight, friends. So it is really important that these activities are done often and integrated throughout your day.

The beauty of letter learning is that, with 26 letters to know (52 if you count each uppercase and lowercase letter!), the games and play can continue for quite some time. And each success—each letter learned— is something to be celebrated along the way!

S-S-S-S-SOUNDING IT ALL OUT

Tomato, tomaaahto. Potato, potaaaahto. Or something like that.

Phonics study is a whole lot cooler than many of us remember it from our own school days. Gone are the days of grainy dittos and boring phonics workbooks where we matched pictures and letters or copied spelling patterns over and over again. Now research shows us that there are a gazillion other exciting and hands-on ways of helping our kids learn the basics of *phonics*, which is really just understanding that there are specific relationships between written letters and spoken sounds. Teachers call this the *alphabetic principle*, which sounds serious. And it is serious business—it's the basis of decoding, or sounding out, words. But it definitely doesn't have to be boring, as you'll see in this chapter.

 TIP #44 MAKE LETTER LEARNING PERSONAL WITH A DIY ALPHABET BOOK.

One of the things parents can do that no classroom teacher can is target everything in every lesson to one child. When you engage your child in these learning activities, you can make the learning all about him or her. Young children are very self-centered, and using that intrinsic quality can be a wonderful trick to inspire learning.

Creating personalized alphabet books is a simple way to work on letter identification as well as letter sounds. Making them is easier than you think.

For a low-tech version, simply cut out pictures of things and places your child loves from magazines or catalogs—flowers, the park, favorite toys, or food. You can supplement these clippings with photos of family, friends, and specific events, such as camping trips, birthday parties, or the day the new baby came home. Try to find at least one picture for each letter of the alphabet. Then on each page, write the uppercase and lowercase letter and paste in your personalized picture. Put the pages together, add a cover with your child's name on it—*Zoe's Alphabet Book*—and you have your very own alphabet book!

For those of you who are tech savvy, there are many options. Snap photos of everyday objects in your home—toys, clothes, furniture,

Five minutes here and there, and your kids will be a few steps closer to knowing the phonics they need to be strong little readers.

pets. People make good subjects too. Try to find something for each letter of the alphabet. If you have a printer, print out the pictures, label them with the appropriate uppercase and lowercase letter, and put the pages together as a book. If you want to get real techy, you can use an online photo editing tool, like www.picmonkey.com or www.canva.com, to make collages of multiple items for each page. You can also use photo-book publishers, like Snapfish, Mixbook, or Shutterfly, to make a bound alphabet book. Let's be clear: Fancy images and a bound book vs. a printed-at-home book won't make a lick of difference in what your child learns. The key is the personalization and the time you take to read it with your child.

Now the fun begins! After you create the book, you have to USE it. Read it together. As you read the words on the cover, *Noah's Alphabet Book*, point to each word. And then as you turn the page, say the letter and the sound it makes, and then point to each picture and say its name. For example, for letter *B*, you might say, "B, *buh, bear, bunny, boxes, blue.*" After you read it, have your child read it. Eventually we want children to take the lead and "read" independently, but in the beginning, this modeling by you is super helpful!

Say each letter name and ask your child what sound it makes. Name the objects and ask your child to tell you the name of the letter each begins with. Ask your child to tell you a story about a photograph. Make it active: Have your child hunt around the house for the objects in the book to turn reading time into a physical activity and deepen their learning even more.

TIP #45 PLAY THE LETTER-SOUND GAME: "SAY IT, SPRAY IT!"

We all know that kids are far too sedentary these days. So why not combine outside time with some letter-sound learning?

Grab some sidewalk chalk and a spray bottle. (We told you this was going to be fun!) Trust us, your child will love it and won't even know that he or she is working hard on developing some seriously awesome reading skills.

Write out letters all over the sidewalk. Fill up the spray bottle with water. Let the fun begin!

To play:

1. Call out single sounds—not the letter name but the sound the letters make. So for *P* just call out /p/ (*puh*).

2. Start with letter sounds your child hears often, like the letters in his or her name. Then challenge your child with sounds not mastered yet.

3. Have your child spray water over the letter that corresponds with the sound you call out.

Next Steps

Call out words and have your child identify and spray the letter that stands for the beginning sound. If you yell *alligator*, your child would spray the *a*. For *heart*, your child sprays the *h*, and so on.

A word of caution: Stay away from words that start with two letters that combine to make the beginning sound. These could be digraphs (two letters that make one sound like, *sh* in *shop* or *ch* in *chart*) or blends

You can also write letters on other outdoor surfaces, such as a fence, and use a hose instead of a spray bottle.

(two letters that work together to make a blended sound like *tr* in *tree* or *sl* in *slide*). It is wise to stick to the single letter, single sounds for now.

With this activity, your child is developing letter-sound knowledge as well as discerning beginning sounds.

 **PUT THOSE MAGNETIC LETTERS TO WORK!**

Magnetic letters can be super-powerful in helping kids learn letter sounds, but you actually have to use them. Oftentimes, parents think they *should* have magnetic letters because they saw another friend use them, and as long as their child sometimes touches them, moves them around, or makes masterpieces out of the letters, then it's all good. Sorry, but magnetic letters only work when they're used as *more* than just a way to keep your child's artwork on the fridge.

Consider using them to:

★ Teach and learn family names

★ Show the difference between uppercase and lowercase letters

★ Practice sorting—sort uppercase letters from lowercase; letters of names from other letters, letters with circles from letters with lines, etc.

★ Play "Can You Find It?" Place 10 to 20 letters in the middle of the fridge and say: *Can you find the* B *or the* P? *Let's look for the uppercase and lowercase* M! *Can you find the* S *or the* T?

★ Celebrate one new word a day (or week!)

★ Practice name spelling

★ Sing the "ABC Song" as you point to each letter

★ Leave secret messages for each other

★ Play "Can You Hear It?" Have 5–10 letters in the middle of the fridge and say, "*Can you find the letter that makes the /b/ or /m/ sound? The /k/ or /l/ sound?*"

★ Play "Can You Hear It?" but experiment with combinations of letters—*sh, th, ch; sl, bl, cl;* or *sm, cr, fr*

★ Reverse the sound games and have your child quiz you

The possibilities are endless. But the bottom line is you have to use those magnets!

TIP #47   LET KIDS PLAY WITH THEIR FOOD.

Surprisingly, there are tons of foods on the market today in the shapes of letters. Get some and give them to your child.

Whether it's snack time or mealtime, kids love to see their names in lights. Or at least in alphabet crackers.

You can find alphabet letters in:

★ crackers

★ cereal

★ noodles

★ soup

★ tater tots

★ cookies

★ and more!

And if you aren't keen on any of the above letter-food options, you can buy alphabet cookie cutters and cut letters out of cheese, fruit, or your own bread. If you want a longer message, use edible color markers (seriously, they do exist!) and write messages on bread and crackers.

Or get creative. Amy's favorite snack growing up was one of her dad's specialties: ring bologna and mustard. Except her dad wouldn't just slap plain ole yellow mustard on ring bologna slices—he'd draw with mustard! She'd get hearts, smiley faces, and, best of all, the first letter of her name. Way to go, Dad!

Remember, though, we not only want to play with letter identification here, we also want to combine letters and sounds. So when you arrange your child's name in crackers and put it on a plate in front of him or her, talk about the sounds that those letters make.

Take the name "Ruby," for example. You can say things like:

★ *Rrrrrrrrruuuuubbbbbyyyy!* (Point to each letter as you emphasize the sounds)

★ *I hear the /r/ sound at the beginning of your name, thanks to the letter* R!

★ *Can you point to the letter* b *when you hear me say the /b/ sound? Ready? Ruby!*

 ## USE LETTER STAMPS WITH PLAY DOUGH!

Play dough is one of our very favorite learning materials, and it's not just for preschoolers.

Believe it or not, play dough can also be used as a phonics-learning and word-building tool. All you need to add are some letter stamps.

Here is a fun and simple way you can build phonics skills with play dough and letter stamps:

1. Gather some play dough and a set of letter stamps.

2. Roll out your play dough into little ovals and stamp out the word-family endings of a common word family (such as –at, -op, -ar, etc.) on three or four different pieces of play dough, leaving space for your child to add a letter at the start of the word.

   When you are done, each piece of play dough should have the same word-family ending on it.

   The best part about using play dough for this activity—mistakes are temporary, but the learning is not!

3. Hand your child the letter stamps so he or she can build words by adding different consonants to the empty space at the beginning of the word. You may end up with *pat, jat, gat*, and *hat* for the *-at* family. Review each word with your child by reading each one and asking, *"Is that a word we use?"* It's totally fine if the word is a nonsense word because kids are working on how words sound. Once they determine it's a nonsense word, have them squish the first letter and replace it with a new one.

Here are the most common word families: *-ack, -ain, -ake, -ale, -all, -ame, -an, -ank, -ap, -ash, -at, -ate, -aw, -ay, -eat, -ell, -est, -ice, -ick, -ide, -ight, -ill, -in, -ine, -ing, -ink, -ip, -it, -ock, -oke, -op, -ore, -ot, -uck, -ug, -ump, -unk*

(Richard E. Wylie and Donald D. Durrell, 1970. Teaching vowels through phonograms. Elementary English, 47, 787-791.)

Choose a family, and let the fun begin!

BUILD WORDS.

There are two important things to keep in mind when it comes to playing with words and sounds:

1. Start with what your child knows.

2. Keep sessions short and sweet.

Here are a few ideas to *really* use letters in ways that will help your child better understand letter sounds and words, stat! Either grab a pencil and paper or a few magnetic letters.

Simply choose a word that your child already knows and then start building. It might look something like this:

Parent: Hey, Mia, do you want to see something cool I can do with a word? I can really shake it up in a super-simple way. Like magic, I can make one thing turn into many. Are you ready for it? It's cool. All I need is one word. Your choice.

Child: What? I don't believe you. Okay. How about *pig?*

Parent: Easy. (Grabs magnetic letters to spell *pig*) Watch me. (Grabs an *s*) Are you ready for this? One pig will magically turn into many by simply adding an . . . *s!* I turned *pig* into *pigs!*

Some other ways to build words:

★ Add a new letter or letters to the word: *look / looked; cat / cats; walk / walking*

★ Change the first letter of the word: *dad / sad; to / do; bell / sell*

★ Change the last letter of the word: *mom / mop; hit / his; top / tot*

★ Add a new letter or letters to the beginning of the word: *at / hat; and / stand; or / for*

★ Change the middle (vowel) of the word: *get / got; man / men; went / want*

★ Put the word together with another word to make a *new* word: *in + to = into; dog + house = doghouse; can + not = cannot*

★ Take a part of two words your child knows to make a totally new word: *sh / she + op / top = shop; pl / play + an / can = plan*

Don't hold back. Feel free to really get wild and crazy. Be excited about how cool and magical words are and can be. And here's where the phonics comes in: Letters have sounds, and letters have power. By adding one little *s* to the end of *cat*, we went from one cat to many!

Whether it's with play dough or magnetic letters, with a spray bottle or an alphabet book, or even with food, give your child opportunities each day to play with letters and the sounds they make—you'll be glad you did!

Many highly regarded reading programs follow the same basic word-building principles, but these activities are based on the Making & Breaking element of the Reading Recovery program (readingrecovery.org).

LOOK WHO'S LEARNING TO READ!

Five minutes here and there. Find the time and you will be making a big difference.

Read it, baby.

Reading is a whole lot tougher than we'd like to admit. Think about it: Beginning readers not only need to learn how to recognize letters in words, but they also need to know the sounds the letters stand for *and* the big picture—comprehension—on top of that. They must learn that when we talk, we use sentences, which are made up of words, which are made up of letters, which make specific sounds when they're put together in certain ways. Bam!

TIP #50 PLAY WITH NAMES.

Before kids reach kindergarten, they should know their names. First, middle, and last. There. We said it.

When Amy was growing up, her parents had these hand-painted, beautiful, framed works of art in the hallway. There was one for each of the four children, and hers said, *Behold your name, Amy. The very first gift from those who gave you life.*

Amy loved this piece of art. Even though she went to school with five other girls named Amy, she grew up knowing that without question, her name was a gift. It was the first gift her parents ever gave her.

Think about it. We spend hours and hours and hours poring over baby-name books and baby-name websites when we're pregnant in an attempt to choose *the* perfect name for our little bean. We write the name, we analyze the initials of the name. Some of us even check out what the monogram might look like (cough). With so much invested in his or her name, it should be the first word you teach your child.

Here are a few fun and easy ways to start getting your child to know and love his or her name:

★ Post your child's name everywhere: on disposable plastic cups so it is visible at breakfast, lunch, and dinner; on the refrigerator; on the walls of his or her room; on the toybox; even on a toothbrush.

★ Really pump up the first letter of your child's name. That first letter is his or her letter. Whenever you see this letter, holler, *HEY! Maddy, can you see that big* M *on the sign? That's your letter!*

It amazes us when we hear kids say they don't know how to spell their name or they aren't sure of their middle name. Really? Let's go, parents. Get on that.

Names are supremely important— often the first words kids read and write! Let's toast to those names— the very first gifts we gave to our little loves.

or *Don't you just love your letter? I mean, that letter* M *is right there at the beginning of your name. It's got a beautiful* mmmmm *sound, and you know what? You'll have it forever!*

★ Always pronounce your child's name correctly, no matter what. Kiddos must hear their names said correctly by the adults in their life. Nicknames are one thing, but their full names? They. Must. Know. How. It. Should. Sound.

★ Make beginning sound connections with your child's name. When you see a neighbor's dog, say, *"Hello, Spot! Hey,* Spot *starts with the same sound as your name,* Sam! Ssspot, Sssam. *Wow–you two are lucky, you both begin with S!"*

★ Talk about the similarities in ending sounds of the names of people you know: *"Listen to how* Mommy *and* Daddy *sound the same at the end. Can you hear it? (Stress the long-e sound.) Who else do we know whose name ends that way?"*

TIP #51 — MIX UP THOSE LETTERS.

Playing with the letters of your child's name is a great way to help him or her learn to spell that name. And really, all kids should know how to spell their names before they get to kindergarten.

You can mix up the letters of a name using just about anything: letter blocks, magnetic letters, letter stickers, foam letters, letter cutouts, or letters on index cards. Depending on the age of your child and length of the name, you could do a number of things.

Start by placing the letters in the correct order, saying, *"This is a very special word for someone I know. I wonder if you know it. This name begins with the letter* M *which makes the* mmmm *sound. It has the letters* M-A-D-E-L-I-N-E *in it. Let me see if I can say this name:* Maaa-duh-lin. *Madeline!"*

By then your child will have probably lit up with excitement. She's excited to learn her name! Why wouldn't she be?

Next, point to each letter as you say its name. Encourage your child to say the letters with you.

Then get a little name nutty. Try any of these activities, beginning with the first, which is the least difficult and gradually moving to the next as your child increases in understanding and confidence.

1. Ask your child to close his or her eyes. While the eyes are closed, take the first letter of the name and put it somewhere in the middle. Say: *Okay. Open your eyes. Something's wrong with this name, and I wonder if you can help me figure out what it is.* Once the child identifies the mixed-up letter, move it back to the front of the name and say: *You got it! That naughty* M *snuck away and went to the wrong place. It belongs in the front of your name because it is the first letter of your name. Then we have the letters...* [say the names of all of the letters]. Do the whole thing again, but this time put the first letter in another place. Rinse and repeat.

2. Take two letters and mix them up. Then put them all back the correct way.

3. Mix up all of the letters of the name.

4. Add three new letters to the mixed-up letters of the name.

5. Add ten new letters to the mixed-up letters of the name.

6. Add all of the letters of the alphabet and see if your child can pick out the letters of his or her name and then put them back in order.

7. Introduce your child's name using an uppercase first letter followed by all lowercase letters, then follow the activities in steps 1–6.

8. Introduce your child's last name using an uppercase first letter followed by all lowercase letters, then follow the activities in steps 1–6.

9. Introduce your child's middle name using an uppercase first letter followed by all lowercase letters, then follow the activities in steps 1–6.

10. Start putting the whole name together whenever your child is ready. Maybe try first name + last name or first name + middle name—go with what you think would be best for your child.

When kids can spell their names, they'll love them even more. They'll really feel like they "own" them once they know *all* of their letters.

TIP #52 FOCUS ON THE PRINT AROUND YOU.

Print is here, there, and everywhere. Teachers call the print that surrounds us "environmental print"—and too often it's overlooked as a learning opportunity for children because many people think that reading "counts" only when it's done between the covers of a book. But that's not the case.

Focusing on environmental print, especially with children, is a fantastic way of letting them know just how important reading really is—it's everywhere! And in order to do just about anything, we have to be able to read!

Make sure you are using what's around you. You can do this by:

★ Reading signs in the doctor's office, the day-care center, church, or anywhere

★ Pointing out street signs

★ Putting a menu in front of your child, pointing to the options as you read, and asking what he or she would like

★ Hanging posters in your home and referring to them during play

★ Creating labels for items in your home

★ Reading billboards or electronic signs in town

★ Identifying the print on cereal boxes or food items

★ Hunting for letters on the license plates of cars

★ Using placemats with letters, words, numbers, or child-friendly concepts

The possibilities are endless! Let's use environmental print every day, everywhere for reading time!

TIP #53 PLAY WITH SIGHT WORDS.

There are some words that kids just need to know. By sight. In fact, there are just 300 words that make up approximately 65% of written language. We call those *high-frequency words*, or *sight words*, because we want kids to know them by sight. That means kids can read them quickly and without thought, within seconds. They need to see the

word and know it so well that they don't even have to think about trying to figure or sound it out.

The reason we want kids to know sight words is because when they commit these words to memory, they can focus more on other words in the text. If kids are hung up on words, such as *is, up, you, and, in, or, the*, or *to*, how can we expect them to have the time, effort, or energy to read everything else?

In addition to high-frequency words, you'll want your child to know his or her own name, family members' names, and pets' names by sight, so add these to the lists we share below.

So as much as possible, as often as possible, once your child is ready, play games with sight words.

This doesn't have to be a huge event. Grab some index cards. Write the following words on the cards: *up, in, at, to, no, did, my, go, said, am, yes, me, like, see, do, on, and, can, is, a, you, he, she, it, are, the, I, look, so, we*.

Once those words are mastered, you can try these: *stop, your, that, from, have, they, made, went, out, come, an, all, saw, but, play, for, get, got, will*.

Always choose two words at one time and give your child an option: *Do you know* [word one] *or* [word two]? *Which would you like to try first,* [word one] *or* [word two]? When we give children options, we're not putting them on the spot, and we're not setting them up for frustration. The work you do with your child at home should be fun, stress-free, and engaging.

Sometimes, there's nothing wrong with staying basic. You can always flip two cards at a time and take turns picking one to read. After the word is read correctly, flip a new card. Or, if you want to mix things up, you can:

★ Let your child read a word into a toy microphone and pass the mic as you take turns

★ Read the word aloud, then build it using magnetic letters on a metal cookie sheet

★ Give your child a tiny chart sticker for each word he or she reads correctly

★ Use a timer to keep track of how fast your child can make it through the stack of word cards

★ Make tally marks for the words your child reads correctly

You can also check out all of the fun ideas in Chapter 8 for making writing fun—just start with the sight-word cards and go from there!

If you write each word on two cards (creating one pair of cards for each word), you can play:

★ Go Fish!

★ Memory

★ Old Maid (Add one extra card and put a funny face on it for the maid.)

Most likely, each year that your child is in school, he or she will receive a new list of words to learn. By the end of each school year, the goal is that your child will have "mastered" each new list. Use some or all of the word-learning activities in this book to help your child learn the words he or she needs to know to succeed in each year of school.

TIP #54) FIND EARLY READER BOOKS YOUR CHILD WILL LOVE.

So your child is getting close to reading on his own (*Yay! This is so exciting!!*), and he wants to give it a go? What should you give him? What can he handle? What should you expect?

First things first: He needs books that are created for just-beginning readers. Teachers call new readers *emergent readers*—and publishers often use that language too. You want to provide your budding reader with a book that will work for him. You want to set him up for success.

The good news is that tons of these books exist. You can usually find them in the "Emergent Reader" section of the library, and many preschools have a lot of these books on hand.

Here are some things you want to look for in emergent books:

★ Simple layout: Each page has a picture or illustration and one or two lines of text

★ Sturdy and small in size, easy for little hands to hold

★ Repetition of words, phrases, layout

★ Interesting, relevant topics

An emergent reader titled *I See* may sound like this: *I see the apple. / I see the tree. / I see the dog. / I see the sunshine. / I see the bus. / I see the house. / I see the car. / I see me!* Each sentence is on its own page with a happy, simple illustration that gives your child a clue about the words. On the *I see the apple* page, you see a picture of an apple; on the *I see a tree* page, a picture of a tree; and so on.

And though these texts might seem a bit boring to us, for your little one, a book like this is fantastic. It is the first book that he or she can read—independently. So it's a huge win.

When you sit down with these books, here's something you can try. Say: *Why don't I read this book first so that you can hear how the words sound? Then when I'm done, I'll hand it to you for you to read to me. We'll take turns. Okay?*

Then read the book out loud, pointing to each word as you read it. In subsequent readings, just point to the final word, the word that varies on each page.

To mix things up a bit, consider doing the following:

★ Say the wrong last word and see if your child corrects you

★ Act like you have forgotten the last word and then sound it out

★ Turn the book upside down or backwards and have your child correct you

It's about combining some skills here—pulling together the print-awareness elements and early word recognition at once. You may be surprised at how well things go!

TIP #55 KNOW HOW TO SUPPORT YOUR CHILD'S EARLY ATTEMPTS AT READING!

You must realize that this point—when kids are almost reading, but not quite, and they still need a ton of support—is a critical time.

We don't want to push kids, and we don't want to stress them, and we don't want to crush their little reading spirits. It's a really important and exciting time, so parents need a playbook.

Here are a few phrases to keep in your back pocket for those times when you're not sure what to do or say.

When your child is stuck on a word, say:

★ *Think about the letters you know and the sounds those letters make. What sounds do these letters make [point to first two letters]? Right. Let's put those two sounds together now.*

★ *Look at the letters you know in the word and at the picture on the page. The picture is here to help you.*

★ *Think about what just happened in the story. You just read* [read previous line]. *Look at the picture, look at the word, and let's take a guess.*

★ *Skip the word that's giving you a hard time and go to the next word you know. We can always come back to this one.*

★ *Maybe you don't recognize this word* [point to the one that caused the stop] *but can you find a part of the word you do know?*

★ *You just read that word on a page before this one. Let's use our strong eyes to see if we can find it to see if that helps.*

When your child makes a mistake during reading, but it's one that doesn't change the meaning of the text, say:

★ Nothing! Let. It. Go. We're trying to build confidence here, and if an error doesn't affect the meaning of the text, there's no need to point it out.

When your child looks up at you after each page for feedback, say:

★ Nothing. Try to get into the habit of just smiling or staying neutral. Don't say, "Good job!" "Great!" or "Nice!" because you want your child to blossom into an independent reader—not one who depends on feedback after every attempt.

When your child makes a reading mistake that *does* change the meaning of the text, say:

★ *Did you read that correctly?*

★ *Read it again and look closely.*

★ *Can you find the tricky part?*

★ If your child can't find the tricky part, then say: *It's in this line.*

★ If your child still can't find it, say: *It's here in this area.*

★ If your child still can't find it, say: *You read* [read the line]. *Which word doesn't match up?*

★ Then go back to the phrases above for when your child is stuck on a word.

When your child says, *But this is a baby book! I don't want to read it!*, say:

★ *Oh, I know you are becoming a really strong reader, but I do want to hear how well you can read this one before we go to the next one. Rereading makes readers more fluent, remember?*

When your child says, *I know this book so well, I can read it with my eyes closed!* (and maybe she really can, since she's memorized it!), say:

★ *Wow! You really do know this book inside and out! How about you point to each word as you read it for me?* or *How about you read it to me one last time in your best reading voice?*

Bottom line? Keep it light and don't become a crutch for your young learner. We want to grow readers who can check their own reading for mistakes, so if you really want to mix things up a bit, you can also ask, *Does that sound right?* even when you know your child has read the words correctly. This will get your child in the habit of checking and re-reading!

So tricky . . . and so helpful!

This is when it gets really exciting, friends—when our children are actually able to read words! With all that has to align, with all of the moving parts when it comes to reading, it's so important that we are right there alongside our children for this learning adventure.

> You don't have to say every single thing perfectly every single time. These responses are initially unnatural for many of us, but we guarantee that they will come more easily with time.

LET'S PUT SOME WRITING ON THAT WALL (OR PAPER, AT LEAST)

Now and again, five minutes at a time, you can help your child build a foundation for strong writing skills.

Put a pen to paper and write, write, write!

When it comes to writing, parents have lots of questions: *When should my child start writing? What should she start writing? Will she automatically know how to hold a pencil? What if she grows up to be "that kid," the one who holds her pencil in a crazy death-grip? Then what?*

Lucky for us, with a little bit of time and a teeny bit of direction, we can help our kids learn how to hold a pencil, take those first few steps in writing letters, and then ultimately become the crazy writing fools they want to be.

TIP #56 — USE SENSORY MATERIALS TO MAKE WRITING FUN.

Writing isn't easy. Adults forget how hard it is because we do it all the time, but we need to remember to make writing fun so that our children want to do it.

You can create letters with so much more than paper and a pencil. When children are first learning to form letters, we encourage parents not to focus too heavily on traditional writing and instead stretch past the paper and pencil to use other, more sensory materials.

Using sensory materials is not just a way to add mess to your beautiful home; it's a way for children to find multiple ways to connect to a new skill. Young children learn with all their senses, so we should be offering them a variety of learning opportunities.

Here are five ways you can help your child work on writing with a sensory approach:

1. **Shaving Cream**
    You can spray it out on a table, but our favorite way to contain the mess is to use a cookie sheet. It doesn't take long for children to see that they can make marks in the shaving cream. Show them that they can use their fingers to form letters, shapes, numbers, and have fun!

2. **Finger Paint**
    Add a generous dollop to a tray or clean cutting board, and have fun. Make letters, then press a paper on top to make a print. This is a simple activity, but your child will love it.

3. **No-Mess Writing Bags**

   Fill a zip-close storage bag halfway with dark colored paint, inexpensive hair gel, or even pudding. Flatten it on a light-colored table (if you don't have one, just slip a sheet of white paper under the bag) and write by gently pressing your index finger onto the bag's surface. Seeing a letter emerge as the color pushes away from the bag is amazing for kids.

4. **Salt/Sugar/Sand Writing**

   We are bunching all three of these items together because the activity is the same; the only difference is the filler—salt, sugar, or sand. Pour your filler about one inch deep in a dish (we like using pie plates), and hand your child a paint brush.

   Let your child create the letters then make them disappear by giving the dish a gentle shake. (Allison uses salt with her kids because they don't like the taste, so they are in no danger of gobbling a handful and getting sick. If you think your kids might try to eat the salt, use sand or sugar instead because salt in large quantities can be dangerous.)

5. **Bendaroos®/ Wikki Stix®**

   These flexible wax-and-wire sticks are wonderful for making letters. They are fun to bend into all different shapes, and children who learn best by making something with their hands can really benefit from using these to form letters and words.

 TIP #57 **BUILD FINE-MOTOR SKILLS TO MAKE WRITING EASIER.**

No one wants to see his or her child struggle. When a child struggles with writing, most parents are inclined to want them to practice, practice, practice.

The thing is, however, that writing isn't a sport. Writing is an important part of literacy that our children need to master. Unlike soccer season, which comes to an end after several weeks, if your child gets burnt out on practicing too much writing, there is no off season.

Instead of burning out your budding writer with repetitive practice, try building his or her fine-motor skills in various fun ways. Here are some suggestions:

Play with lacing cards. You can find lacing cards with all sorts of fun themes, or you can make your own with cardboard, a hole punch, and some shoelaces.

Play with interlocking brick toys. Not only are these toys great for encouraging creativity, they are also one of the best activities for building the motor skills needed for writing.

Play with stickers. This is a great on-the-go activity. Peel the extra backing off the sheets to make it easier for little ones.

Practice using scissors. You can start by letting your child cut play dough with dull or plastic scissors, then work up to child-safe scissors and scrap paper.

Use tweezers and tongs. Have your child pick up pom poms with tweezers and place them into an empty ice tray or other divided container.

Create with a rubber-band loom. This super-popular craft tool is amazing for building hand strength and control. You can wear your kid's creations with pride knowing he or she was also developing fine-motor skills!

String beads. Start little ones off with a chenille stem when beading so that the beads don't slide off and result in major meltdowns. If you have a little dish with a lid, beading can be a great activity to take on the go for waiting rooms, sport sidelines, and road trips.

Knead play dough. Not only is playing with play dough calming, it also builds hand strength! Knead away!

Complete connect-the-dots pictures. This is our secret weapon with kids who proclaim they hate to draw because the picture always turns out the way it should. (It's also a good activity for developing fine-motor skills!)

Lock and unlock padlocks. What? Yes. You'd be surprised how much kids love to do this. Collect locks and give your child a pile of keys to try to find the match. It is a simple activity, but kids go nuts for it!

TIP #58 LET THEM WRITE ON THE WALL— YES, REALLY!

When a girlfriend posted (in exasperation) a photo online of a beautiful piece of artwork that her child created (without permission!) on her cream-colored dining room wall, Allison's first thought was, "That's great for hand strength!"

Allison's comment probably wasn't what her friend was expecting to read, but it's true. Writing on walls and other, more socially acceptable, elevated vertical surfaces, like easels, chalkboards, and whiteboards, is a terrific, low-stress way for children to develop important writing skills. When children write on this type of surface, not only are they developing the correct muscles needed for writing, but their arm and hand will also end up naturally in the correct position. Try it.

Here are seven surfaces you can have your child try:

★ an easel

★ a blackboard attached to the wall

★ a homemade blackboard (made with blackboard paint on the wall)

★ a whiteboard (Mini ones mounted on bedroom doors are always a hit.)

★ windows and glass doors (use window markers)

★ an acrylic document display stand (Place it on a table as a great mini easel!)

★ your wall! (Just be sure to use craft paper and painter's tape, and make it OK only to write on that specific section of the wall!)

Remember that writing begins with scribbles and drawing—scribbling is how a toddler writes, giant letters are perfect three-year-old writing, and so on. So celebrate these early attempts, knowing that your child will eventually move beyond scribbles and will develop printing skills all in good time. What's important now is to acknowledge your child's ability to convey ideas through marks on a page.

TIP #59 FIND THE BEST WRITING TOOLS FOR YOUR CHILD.

Sometimes it's cool to take a few steps back and make sure you've got the best resources for your child.

Whiteboards and other dry-erase writing tools are wonderful. Kids love using them, but if your little writer is having a hard time forming letters, then it makes sense to reassess and choose a different, more appropriate utensil and surface for writing.

The surface of a chalkboard offers more resistance than the dry-erase board, and this is exactly what children who are still working on fine-motor control need. The additional resistance will allow your child to write slower and with more precision. When Allison's son was struggling with letter formation, his kindergarten teacher explained this to her, and when she switched, it was like night and day. Now we share this tip with as many parents as we can!

Many tools exist for children who need more than a regular-sized crayon or pencil for forming letters. Jumbo-sized crayons give kids a bit extra to hold on to, and triangular-shaped crayons make the tripod grip a bit easier to master (see Tip #61).

 **SET UP A SIMPLE WRITING CENTER.**

When we tell other parents that we have a little writing center in our playroom, they either look at us like we are speaking a language they don't understand, or they lean in and ask what it is and whether it was expensive. No, it wasn't expensive and, yes, our children use it—a lot.

Think of a writing center as a cousin to the book nook. It's a fun, inviting place to write. Here are the basics you'll want to include in your writing center:

- ★ fun paper
- ★ pencils, markers, and crayons
- ★ a clipboard
- ★ containers for the writing tools

Pretty simple, but it will get the job done.

You can boost the writing center up a notch by adding word cards, cards of upper- and lowercase letters, family pictures with names and addresses on the back, blank greeting cards, envelopes, stickers, and/or a Magna Doodle™.

Our children use their writing center to write poems, birthday cards for friends, and letters to family far away. The Magna Doodle is used for writing rough drafts—Allison's son came up with this great idea when he wanted to test his spelling before committing it to paper.

As your child discovers that the writing center is a great place to write and create, you can adjust what you put there and switch it up from time to time. When we notice the kids haven't been writing much, we add a few new stickers, scented markers, or something else just a little bit special to the center. Eventually, their interest is renewed.

Great places for a home writing center are kitchen desks, playrooms, home offices, or bedrooms. You can even make it portable!

TIP #61 **TEACH YOUR CHILD THE TRIPOD GRIP.**

Kids need to be taught the proper way to hold a writing utensil. It's not innate.

Most children go through a stage where they grasp the pencil or crayon or marker fisted and for dear life, and that's totally normal. In fact, it's great. We want our children to know that they can control a writing device, and that it's really fun and fulfilling to make marks on a page.

But around the time that your child actually attempts to write letters, it's time to give him or her a little direction. This doesn't have to be a huge, stressful, complex lesson; rather, gently move your child's fingers around the writing utensil so that the pinky and ring fingers are resting on the palm and the thumb and the pointer and middle finger work together to control the utensil.

This grip, where three digits work together harmoniously, is called the "tripod grip." In the event that it's more comfortable for the child to use four fingers to control movement, that's totally fine. We call this four-fingered approach the "quadropod grip."

A few gentle reminders, and your child will have it in no time!

TIP #62 JUMPSTART YOUR CHILD'S WRITING WITH X'S AND O'S!

There really is a logical place to start when you're trying to teach your kids to write, and what we say here may surprise you. When it comes to writing, start simple.

Encourage your child to start writing X's and O's. Put X's and O's everywhere—on paper, on the steamed-up window in the bathroom, on the driveway. Make X's and O's big, small, fat, skinny, plain, and fancy. Draw them with anything and everything: markers, crayons, watercolors, pens—you name it.

Once kids are ready for something new, teach them how to make a square and a triangle.

Mastering these two letters—X and O—and these two shapes—square and triangle—will give your child the basic skills he or she needs to form just about every letter of the alphabet.

And another reason learning X's and O's rocks? Your kids will have learned their very first written message: hugs and kisses.

Put X's and O's and squares and triangles everywhere, and make them in all sorts of sizes and styles, with all sorts of writing tools.

DO SOME SHARED WRITING.

Once kids have a few letters they can create with confidence under their belt, it's time for some shared writing.

Shared writing is just that—writing that is shared between two people. And early shared writing has more to do with helping kids break down sounds and remember letters than it does with actually creating a life-changing novel.

Shared writing often begins with a conversation. At this stage, most emerging readers are chatty and love talking about themselves, so a conversation about their favorite subject— them!—is a great starting point.

Some questions to consider asking your child:

★ *What would happen on your very best day?*

★ *Tell me about a time when you felt really happy.*

★ *If you could do something to surprise me, what would you do?*

★ *Let's take turns sharing stories about a time when we got really, really messy from playing.*

★ *What was the best part of your first day at preschool/Sunday school/dance class?*

★ *Let's talk about our favorite princess/car/animal . . .*

Once you decide on a topic, hand your child the writing utensil and say: *Oh, my goodness, that is such an incredible story. Let's write it down so that we never, ever forget it.*

Do everything you can to let your child take the lead, and do what you can to keep the experience light and easy. Only jump in if your child asks for help. Words will not be spelled correctly, and letters will not be formed perfectly. It's all good.

Anytime your child isn't sure about what letter or letters to write, say:

★ *What sounds do you hear?*

★ *What letter (or letters) makes that sound?*

★ *Let's say the word together slowly to see if we can hear the sounds.*

Take your own pencil and write the word or letters on your paper, large enough for your child to see, and say something like this: *Let me help. The first part of this word is tricky, but I bet you can figure out the last part.*

Or perhaps, *You've written the first part of the word, and the last part looks like this.* (Show the word.) *Now that you know it ends with an* s, *can you hear that in the word when you say it aloud?*

Remember that the writing can be done about any topic, and it can be done for any reason. Shared writing can be used to help a child write a birthday letter to a grandparent or to help a child write a note to a friend. It's not about setting our kids up for a frustrating challenge; we need to let them know that we, as parents, are here to support them in everything—especially reading and writing!

TIP #64 WRITE MORE THAN JUST STORIES.

All writing is real-world writing. Writing a story is just as real as writing a letter to Grandma. They are different types of writing, though, and by a young age, many children have already decided whether they like a certain kind of writing or not. The same way that children will often have a preference between reading fiction and nonfiction texts, some will enjoy writing stories or poetry over thank-you notes and to-do lists.

> If your child is stuck, immediately lend a hand.

The list of writing activities below is for those kids who need more than a stack of paper and an idea in order to get a story on paper (which, by the way, is most kids).

All of these activities can be done by pre-writers and writers alike; children of all ages need to have ample opportunities to practice writing, even if it just looks like scribbles to us. Children can:

- ★ Plan and write a menu for meals
- ★ Write a postcard to a family member far away
- ★ Label toys with the proper name
- ★ Write silly holiday cards for days like "Talk-Like-a-Pirate Day" and "Donut Day"
- ★ Decorate the sidewalk with chalk messages
- ★ Create wish lists (This is a favorite at our house. It blends children's natural desire for gifts and treats with the realistic concept that they are just wishes. It also gets kids writing!)
- ★ Keep a journal or diary (Young children can draw, write, or scribble in their very own journal. Allison's son, who is a much bigger fan of reading than writing, loves writing in his journal!)
- ★ Design signs (Name plates for doors, rules for their bedrooms, playroom reminders—whatever works for your family. Grab some painter's tape and post them on the walls to promote reading, too.)

All writing is real-world writing—so don't feel limited to stories!

From building fine-motor skills to finding the right materials to providing lots of opportunities to practice, there's so much you can do to nurture your child's early writing skills. So put pen (or pencil or crayon or marker) to paper, and get writing!

READING AND TALKING AND THINKING—OH, MY!

Five minutes during your read-aloud is all you need to get your child in the reading zone. You can teach comprehension strategies even before your child is actually reading on her own. Really. It's crazy cool.

Let's do it.

Read-alouds are the big dog. Most parents know they should read to their kids, so they do. This is awesome. Usually the experience is a warm and cozy snuggle time, when a book is read from cover to cover, and you feel like a parent rock star. But sometimes . . . well, not so much.

Sometimes, kids wiggle and move and may not want to sit still, which is why it's so important for parents to set the stage for an engaged and active read-aloud. Sure, you're still able to get all cozy with your little one as you read, but when you're really maximizing a read-aloud, you're doing more than just spending some quality time with your child. You're building a solid foundation for literacy learning even before your child can read on his or her own.

That's right. One of the coolest things about reading is that you can teach your child basic reading comprehension skills even *before* he or she can actually read. You do this—wait for it—during read-alouds.

Modeling strong reading skills as you read a book will do the trick. You will do it so naturally and in such an easy, conversational way that your child won't even realize that she is working or learning. And you do it so frequently that it becomes a habit for you both. So that any time your child is listening to *you* read a book, *her* little brain is working. She's making predictions. She's making connections. She's asking questions. She's visualizing.

And when your child is able to read on her own, these strategies will come naturally and effortlessly.

 TIP #65 ## THINK OUT LOUD.

Our kids look up to us and admire us, that we know. They want to wear what we wear, eat what we eat, and do what we do. (At least while they're still young!)

So it's natural that they'd be interested in knowing what we are thinking about as well. And we can share what we're thinking any time of the day, of course, but it has more benefits in terms of literacy when we share our thoughts about what we're reading. That's what "think-alouds" are: shared thinking. Thinking out loud.

Thinking aloud is super simple. Almost any thoughts you share count, including comments on story elements—like setting, characters, and conflict—or on the book's layout—like the photos, illustrations, or style of print.

Think-alouds actually demonstrate to kids how strong readers process what they read. They show kids how they, too, should interact with text once they become fluent readers.

Some examples might be:

★ *Oh, I love the other books that Marc Brown has written. I wonder if I'll like this one as much.*

★ *Right off the bat I can tell that the blanket is going to be a problem for Owen.*

★ *Hmmm. I wonder why Jack and Annie glanced at each other when Merlin said that.*

★ *Junie should not talk like that to her mother! I don't appreciate her sass!*

★ *I am closing my eyes right now, trying to imagine that I can taste the apple pie they just made.*

★ *Look at the way the print is laid out on this page. I love that it looks like a pyramid. So unusual.*

TIP #66 — READ TO MODEL FLUENT READING.

Kids need to hear how fluent reading sounds.

Fluent reading is reading that sounds natural and conversational. It is not too fast and not too slow. It has a relaxed cadence and is delivered in a comfortable volume. When you model fluent reading, you use expression to show emotion, speed up at exciting parts, slow down at spooky parts, and pause dramatically to create suspense. You can even try out different voices for different characters. All these variations in reading rate and tone demonstrate that you understand what's going on in the story and are paying attention to the punctuation—exactly what we want kids to do when they start reading on their own.

Modeling fluent reading is important because when kids first start reading themselves, it's usually a slow, laborious process. They start

and stop to carefully sound out words, and/
or stumble on punctuation. And that is how it
begins. But we show them what reading can be
by letting them hear us read fluently, so take
every chance you can to read aloud to your child.
Not only will you—and your child—appreciate
the time together, but you'll also be doing your
beginning reader a big service by letting him or
her hear how fluent reading should sound.

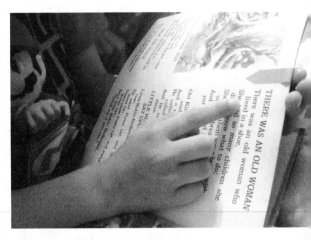

If you are not a fluent reader, or if you are not
comfortable with your own reading skills, don't
worry. Support your child with the help of audiobooks. Nearly every
library has an audiobook section, and allowing children to listen while
they follow along in the book is a great way for them to enjoy a text, to
learn new words, and to hear fluent reading at the same time.

Audiobooks are also a great time-saver on those extra-busy days—pop
one in while you're cooking dinner or driving to practice, and your child
gets some of the benefit of a read-aloud even when you just can't fit in
the reading yourself.

TIP #67   ACTIVATE SCHEMA.

You may not think much about schema, but you use it all day, every
day—and so does your child. We like to think of our *schemata* (plural of
schema) as a file cabinet full of information about everything we know
that's stored in our brain. When you "activate schema," you're pulling
one manila folder of information out of that file cabinet.

Some teachers call this "activating prior knowledge." It's a different
phrase for the same thing. Before we start reading a text with our

children, we activate schema so that they can more clearly understand and remember what they're reading. Just as when we're building words, we begin with what we know and go from there. Same deal.

For example, before reading *Up, Up, Up! It's Apple-Picking Time* by Jody Fickes Shapiro, we might recall and chat about the preschool field trip to the apple orchard. We're pulling out that manila folder full of apple orchard information so that it's ready to support and clarify what we're about to read.

Before we pick up *Too Many Pumpkins* by Linda White, chatting about what we know about pumpkins, their seeds, and their ability to grow in just about any condition, will help us to really, truly understand why Rebecca Estelle ends up with more pumpkins than she can believe. It will help us to better understand and appreciate Rebecca Estelle's hard work in carving so many pumpkins and her kind and generous spirit in preparing pumpkin dishes to feed all of her friends. Connecting to his or her own knowledge about pumpkins allows the reader to think critically about the text as well and to answer difficult questions, such as:

★ Is it possible for an entire yard to be filled with pumpkins if only one pumpkin splattered its seeds in the grass?

★ Could one person really do all that this character did—move hundreds of pumpkins from the yard to the house, carve them, and cook them? Why or why not?

★ Why would the author choose to make these choices? What message is the author trying to send to readers?

Activating schema is one of those things that can take just a minute (a quick conversation about a memory or experience) or can last much longer (carefully looking at photo albums, examining souvenirs, or watching short videos), but depending on your purpose and the text at hand, either way it can pack a powerful punch for reading comprehension.

MAKE CONNECTIONS.

Making connections is usually one of the first reading comprehension strategies that children do naturally when reading a text, since most young ones *looove* to talk about themselves.

Connecting lets readers relate directly to the characters, events, or ideas in a text. When readers are able to create a connection to a text, they're more likely to remember what they're reading, and they often understand it at a deeper level. For instance, if you're reading *A Weekend With Wendell* by Kevin Henkes, maybe your child has had a similar experience with an unwelcome guest and can truly empathize with Sophie's trials. If your child has a favorite stuffed animal, like Trixie of *Knuffle Bunny* by Mo Willems, then he or she will totally understand how Trixie must feel when she loses her beloved bunny.

During read-alouds, you can model connection-making by making comments like:

★ *The grandmother in this story reminds me of my own grandma because my grandma told stories about what life was like when she was a little girl.*

★ *Trixie seems really attached to Knuffle Bunny, doesn't she? I know a few other kids who take their lovies everywhere.*

★ *Oh boy. This boy's blue face reminds me of Violet Beauregarde in Charlie and the Chocolate Factory. I hope his manners are better than hers.*

★ *Remember how the girl in* The Gardener *sent letters to her family while she was away? The little boy in this book does something similar.*

Our hope is that when beginning readers—and even toddlers or preschoolers—hear adults frequently making connections to their own lives or other books as they read, that the little ones, too, will make connections when *they* are the ones doing the reading. Very simply, we're hoping that our kids will pick up on the habits of strong readers early on, and then they will naturally use these strategies on their own when they're able.

 TIP #69 **MAKE MOVIES IN YOUR MIND.**

Many educators firmly believe visualization is the key to reading success. We don't argue with them. Visualizing *is* crazy important.

When kids can picture in their minds what's happening in the story, then they have a clear understanding of what's going on. If you stop every so often during a read-aloud to share "mind movies," you will be able to tell whether your child has a firm grasp of the content.

Though many picture books today are complete with rich and vivid illustrations that aid children in creating these mind movies, it's worth stopping for a bit to talk about visualization. There will be times when your child is only listening and not looking at pictures, such as when the teacher reads at the front of the room, when the child is listening to audiobooks, or when the child starts exploring chapter books that have fewer photos or illustrations.

If you encounter a passage filled with imagery in a book or magazine, point it out. Say, *Oh I love how the author described this kitchen. The words she chose make me feel like I can see the dough rising, smell the bread*

> Being able to visualize what's being read is muy importante for comprehension.

baking, and see them sharing the warm slices at the table. Close your eyes and, as I read, listen closely to the words and see the movie in your mind.

Let mind movies become a regular topic in your house. You'll enjoy this little glimpse into the way your child's mind works.

 **MAKE PREDICTIONS.**

Predicting is one of the easiest comprehension strategies to use with beginning readers, and like many of these important early literacy skills, predicting can be taught *even before* children can read on their own.

Predicting as a reading strategy is actually just using pictures or text to make a guess about what will happen. Even our little ones can do this by looking at the cover of a book or the illustrations on a page, or by hearing the title read aloud.

You can model predicting very simply:

- ★ Look at the cover of the book, read the title and the back cover, and flip through the book to examine the illustrations, chapter titles, and other clues, then share what you think the story will be about.
- ★ Stop to check on your prediction after a few pages. Were you correct? Say so! Were you wrong? Explain how surprised you are at the change!

Predicting is cool because it can be used with just about anything, including just about any children's book. It also keeps children engaged in the reading because they wonder if what they think will happen actually does. (They'll feel like little detectives!)

Predicting helps children remember what they've read and makes them better readers and thinkers!

ASK QUESTIONS.

Questioning is queen (at least in our book).

Reading is an active process; from start to finish, the reader is working to construct meaning from the words written on the page. One thing that will really help kids become stronger readers is questioning.

Questioning is just that: asking questions about the reading. When readers can ask logical questions about characters, setting, plot, or other story elements, they are:

★ more engaged

★ more invested

★ more active listeners

★ more likely to remember what's being read

Questions can obviously come in a multitude of forms, but here are a few question starters that you can use as you think aloud with your child:

★ *I wonder why . . .*

★ *Where did he . . .*

★ *Why did that character . . .*

★ *When will they . . .*

★ *If he goes . . .*

★ *Who will help the . . .*

★ *What will they do if . . .*

★ *Why did they decide to . . .*

When kids get older, teachers may have them write their questions on sticky notes and put them on the related pages. Not only is that a great way to keep older readers engaged and actively reading, but it also reminds them to revisit the question—to see whether or not all questions will be answered in a text.

So, though you don't need to go as far as to write down your questions during read-alouds, do try to address your questions as you read. And

> Some questions will remain unanswered through a book; the author leaves it up to the reader to decide. Talk about that! Share some ideas about why an author may do this and then consider some possible answers to any unanswered question.

make a big deal about finding the answers—it's exciting when kids engage with a story this way, so make a big fuss when you find the answer.

This early type of book talk is so much fun and so interesting. You may be surprised at how insightful and thoughtful your child can be!

TIP #72   SUMMARIZE.

Oooooooh, boy, summaries can be difficult. When we summarize, we bring together information. We pull together all the important parts and share them in a way that is understandable and simple—which is why summaries can be so difficult. Especially for kids.

To help kids learn this all-important skill, we start them with the One-Hand Summary, a simple trick for picking out the main points of a reading and sharing them in no more than five sentences. Kids can keep count on their one hand; if the summary exceeds five sentences, then it is too long.

How does the One-Hand Summary work? Each finger stands for a key idea that should be included in a summary:

1. *In this story . . .*

2. *Someone . . .*

3. *Wanted/Thought . . .*

4. *But then . . .*

5. *Finally . . .*

Here's a fantastic summary of *Pop's Bridge* by Eve Bunting, using the One-Hand Summary: *In* Pop's Bridge *by Eve Bunting, Robert thought that his father had the most important job in building the Golden Gate Bridge in*

California. But then there was a bad accident on the bridge. Finally, Robert realizes that every job on the bridge is important.

That's a pretty sweet summary. If you look closely, you'll see it covers all the essentials:

★ In this story: We even mention the title and author here, but you don't have to. We just want kids to get into the habit of introducing their thoughts in the clearest way possible to prepare them for creating topic sentences in paragraph writing.

★ Someone: *Robert*, one of the main characters

★ Wanted/Thought: *... thought that his father had the most important job in building the Golden Gate Bridge in California.*

★ But then: *... there was a bad accident on the bridge.*

★ Finally ... : *Robert realizes that every job on the bridge is important.*

Hooray! This summary definitely fits on one hand—it is only three sentences, so three fingers!

Creating a proper summary takes work and a lot of practice, but kids should understand that summaries should not be more than five sentences long (one for each finger) and should contain only facts (no opinions!).

> We want to really stress the importance of keeping summaries concise and factual. And using those fingers is a great reminder that there shouldn't be more than five sentences in a summary.

The great thing about all of these read-aloud strategies is that not one requires our kids to be doing the actual reading! However, each one still reinforces really important reading comprehension skills. That means that in just a small amount of time, with just a little bit of focus, we are helping our kids to become stronger readers!

TIME TO GET TECHY

Kids are toddling around today with their parents' cell phones in one hand and a bottle in the other. Look around any restaurant or waiting room, and you'll see half a dozen kids swiping through games and apps while their parents do the same on their own devices.

But what's on that device that is worth your kids' time? How are parents expected to plow through the trillions of apps on the market to find the ones that really count? How do parents know which television program is worth introducing to their children or which characters should be invited into their home? Ones that promote literacy learning and make it fun? We got it.

Let's do what we can to rein in screen time and technology use so our kids can become the digital kids they're destined to be, but build the skills they need to become strong *unplugged* readers as well.

TIP #73 BE INTENTIONAL WITH TECHNOLOGY.

Technology is a part of our children's life. While many of us remember when we got our first computer, most of our kids won't remember life before smart phones.

Our children engage with technology almost daily in numerous ways, and they will be expected to be competent users as they grow. So as much as we may want to shield them from technology—especially at a young age—they are still surrounded by it.

Therefore, we feel that the best thing to do when it comes to helping parents integrate technology into their child's literacy skill development is to create some basic guidelines to think about when making TV, movie, app, and gaming decisions.

Consider using these questions to guide your decisions:

- ★ Does this program or app encourage my child to research a topic or seek out reading materials about the subject?

- ★ Do you and your child discuss the material during or after watching the program?

- ★ What kind of new vocabulary is my child learning from this app or program?

- ★ Does my child play creatively with toys using ideas or concepts from these programs or apps?

- ★ Does viewing the program or using the app involve reading of any sort?

- ★ Are the graphics and images visually appealing?

- ★ Is the creator or developer a trusted, reliable resource?

Literacy development and technology can work together beautifully when done intentionally. If ever you have questions about a certain app or program, we suggest checking out a reliable site like Common Sense Media (www.commonsensemedia.org/), where books, programs, movies, and apps are reviewed on a regular basis.

The American Academy of Pediatrics recommends no more than two hours of entertainment screen time a day for children ages 3–18 (pediatrics.aappublications.org/content/132/5/958.full), discouraging any screen media exposure for children two years and younger. We definitely suggest talking to your pediatrician about the guidelines that he or she suggests, but we believe that, as in everything, moderation and choice is key.

 **USE TECHNOLOGY AS A TREAT.**

Screen time is a big deal at our house. Our kids are completely aware that their screen time is limited, and that fact alone has turned it into a very coveted treat—like ice cream or the rare soda at a birthday party.

Use that to your advantage, and use e-books, literacy apps, and audio books as treats, too.

In our house, a child gets a choice of reading on the tablet for 35 minutes vs. 20 minutes of doing something passive, like watching a cartoon.

While traveling, we bring a tablet on the plane or in the car and fill it up with new literacy-focused apps. The novelty of a new app coupled with extended screen time is a win-win. Kids are working on their literacy skills and replacing time where they might otherwise put their brain on a shelf with time spent productively engaged.

> It's up to parents to make sure that any guidelines are adhered to and that children are provided with smart programming choices.

Only you know the right formula for your child, but we encourage you to search out literacy apps and download some e-books for a treat!

What should you look for in the e-books and apps you choose? Make sure that they are relatively distraction-free, and:

- ★ do not require in-app purchases
- ★ maintain the integrity of the original text (if the e-book is based on a traditional book)
- ★ are easy for children to use
- ★ have a "read-to-me" feature where the word being read is highlighted
- ★ are high-quality stories
- ★ contain appealing graphics

TIP #75 CHOOSE THE BEST APPS AND WEBSITES.

The good news is that being inundated with apps and websites means we can be choosy. And when it comes to our kids, we *should* be choosy—especially with screen time.

So how do you determine the best device, app, or website for your child? We don't have all the answers, but we can tell you how we make our decisions, and we can share with you a handful of our favorites. There's no right answer here, and what works for one family may not work for another. But essentially, the following apps and websites have proven that they work for our kids.

Our favorite apps for the little ones:

iWriteWords: Beginning writers learn how to form letters in this interactive app.

Speakaboos Stories: Here, songs, videos, books, and interactive applications are all based on books and storytelling.

Learn With Homer: All elements of early literacy are covered in a visually appealing app.

Starfall Learn to Read: Just like the site (www. starfall.com), this app covers all bases of learning to read in fun and engaging ways.

Cookie Doodle: Encourages cookie baking (via app!) and recipe reading.

Articulation Station: Teaches children how to pronounce English sounds in fun and engaging activities.

Our favorite apps for slightly older kids:

American Girl: Kanani, McKenna, Saige, and many of the heroines of the American Girl stories have apps that support their stories.

SpellingCity: Straight from the popular site by the same name, this app contains great tools for learning spelling and vocabulary words.

BrainPOP® Jr: This video encyclopedia app is filled with information about all topic areas.

Word Mover: From www.readwritethink.org, this app allows users to create poems and messages with "magnetic words."

More Breakfast: Build a mouth-watering breakfast while reading ingredients.

Weird but True!: From National Geographic Kids, users swipe the screen for fact after fact, each one stranger than the next.

Have questions about programming for kids? Ask some trusted friends what they share with their children, or ask your child's teacher for a list of recommendations.

Our favorite websites for kids:

★ Sesame Workshop (www.sesameworkshop.org)

★ ABCmouse (www.abcmouse.com)

★ Starfall.com (www.starfall.com)

★ VocabularySpellingCity (www.spellingcity.com)

★ PBS Kids (pbskids.org/)

★ NatGeo Kids (kids.nationalgeographic.com)

★ Disney Junior (disneyjunior.disney.com)

★ Smithsonian Kids (www.si.edu/Kids)

★ PBS LearningMedia (pbslearningmedia.org)

Check out the above recommendations thoroughly yourself first, and then introduce them to your child slowly and patiently. Children are likely to catch on quickly, but they should never be unsupervised while playing online.

We know it's not easy to do this parenting thing—it's the most difficult job out there, and that's a fact! But one thing that we want all parents to know is that if you try to incorporate even one of these early literacy tips into your child's day, the payoff will be huge. Your child will be a stronger reader from the start and will be well on the way to becoming a lifelong reader.

Begin small: Set the goal of trying one tip the first week. Then try two of our tips the next week. Then shoot for three tips the following week. Before you know it, adding one of our quick tips to your daily schedule will be a cinch! What are you waiting for, friends? Get started, and enjoy reading!